"Why hasn't anybody ever written a little book like this before? First-year Greek students should read it. Exegesis students should read it. Preachers who have had a year or two of Greek should read it. And it's so short and straightforward, the same person should read it in all three capacities. Do what Con Campbell says and you *will* keep your Greek. But don't just believe him; read the exchanges from his blogsite, which he includes that prove it!"
—CRAIG L. BLOMBERG, Distinguished Professor of
New Testament, Denver Seminary, Littleton, CO

"Rightly does Campbell insist that Christian teachers and preachers need to keep their Greek going, and shrewdly does he spell out the ways and means of doing that."
—J. I. PACKER, Professor of Theology, Regent College

"*Keep Your Greek* is a godsend. It's chock-full of wit, humor, and good advice. Campbell's approach is practical—and achievable. With all the tools available to us today, it only takes a little discipline to get your Greek back. One professor exhorted his charges that it is a great 'sin and loss that we do not study [the biblical] languages, especially in these days when God is offering and giving us men and books and every facility and inducement to this study, and desires his Bible to be an open book.' The professor was Martin Luther, nearly 500 years ago! How much less of an excuse do we have today? Campbell ties together the reasons and the approach, the motivation and the principles, to keep your Greek. He drives home his message with a velvet-wrapped sledge hammer. You will feel convicted, challenged, and most of all encouraged to get back into the game."
—DANIEL B. WALLACE, Professor of New Testament
Studies, Dallas Theological Seminary

CONSTANTINE R. CAMPBELL

KEEP YOUR
GREEK

STRATEGIES FOR BUSY PEOPLE

ZONDERVAN®

ZONDERVAN.com/
AUTHORTRACKER
follow your favorite authors

We want to hear from you. Please send your comments about this book to us in care of zreview@zondervan.com. Thank you.

ZONDERVAN

Keep Your Greek
Copyright © 2010 by Constantine R. Campbell

This title is also available as a Zondervan ebook. Visit www.zondervan.com/ebooks.

Requests for information should be addressed to:

Zondervan, *Grand Rapids, Michigan 49530*

Library of Congress Cataloging-in-Publication Data

Campbell, Constantine R.
    Keep your Greek: strategies for busy people / Constantine R. Campbell.
      p. cm.
    ISBN 978-0-310-32907-7 (pbk.)
    1. Greek language, Biblical. I. Title.
PA810.C36 2010
487'.4 – dc22   2010012126

Cover design: *Chris Tobias*
Interior design: *Matthew VanZomeren*

Printed in the United States of America

HB 03.11.2024

CONTENTS

Introduction

GREEK MAKES A DIFFERENCE

Struggling to Keep Your Greek?

I teach Greek at Moore College in Sydney, Australia. One of the most common questions I am asked by current and former students is: *What are your tips for keeping my Greek going after college?* Most of our students go into ministry after studying at Moore, though not all do. Whatever they end up doing, however, they know that they will have a lot less time to work on their Greek once they leave. How realistic will it be to maintain the knowledge they've acquired? Will they be able to keep up their Greek skills? Won't ministry be so busy, with so many other things that need doing, that Greek will get squeezed out?

I've chatted with many people already in ministry — some only for a year or two, and others a decade or two — who have shared how difficult it has been to keep their Greek. It seems that the fears of my students have been realized by many of the men and women who are already out there. Some guys have completely lost their Greek. Others are clinging on to it, but they have lost a lot of the details. Some others have managed to maintain their skills, but it's been hard work and a constant struggle. Only a few seem to have actually advanced their ability with Greek and taken their skills and knowledge to new levels.

Well, that all sounds pretty depressing, doesn't it?

As a teacher of Greek, it's natural for me to think about this problem. Of first importance, I want my students to keep their Greek skills over the long term, for the sake of their understanding of the New Testament and for their ability to teach the New Testament to others. It's a ministry thing. Of secondary importance (a distant second), I don't want my teaching to be a waste of time and effort! I have to admit it's been pretty demoralizing to hear that some former students have given up on Greek.

A few years ago, I started sharing some tips in my classes about how to keep up with Greek over the long term. I figured that my students could put some simple habits and attitudes into practice now that would serve them long after they left college. That seemed to be a helpful step. Next, I began a series called "Keep your Greek" on my blog (http://readbetterpreachbetter.com). There were nine posts in the series, with one tip per post. I was surprised by how much interest and feedback there was, gauged by the responses to the blog posts, though I suppose I shouldn't have been surprised. There are plenty of people out there who are struggling to keep their Greek, and many are looking for help.

Those blog posts have since become the outline for this book, and I've turned the original nine blog posts into the first nine chapters (I've added new material too, in case you're wondering). I've also included the comments and questions that the original blog posts generated because I think it's helpful to hear the reactions of others to some of my ideas and suggestions. I don't necessarily agree with everything my blog readers have said, but their comments may be of help to you (and some of them are good for a laugh!). I also think that this is a topic best discussed in community, and the comments help to reflect that vibe.

Why Keep Your Greek?

Most people reading this will not need to be persuaded of the value of keeping their Greek. The whole reason they're reading this now is to find some help to do just that. But others may not be convinced just yet, so it's worth outlining why keeping your Greek is worth the time and effort.

If you're a teacher of God's Word, the main reason to keep your Greek is the same reason that led you to study it in the first place. Greek gives us certain insights into the text of the New Testament that are impossible to achieve any other way. This goes well beyond looking up particular words in the original, even though that is useful. It includes understanding the syntax and structure of sentences, so that we can discern what the author is drawing attention to and how all the parts relate to each other. It includes understanding the nuances of case, mood, tense, and voice, so that we can appreciate what the Greek means even if its full meaning cannot be translated into English. It gives us access to exegetical and theological debates, so that we can think for ourselves about the text, rather than rely solely on commentaries. It gives us access to the world of the text, so that we can be immersed in what was actually written two thousand years ago, pure and unadulterated.

Keep your Greek for your own understanding of God's Word.

These great insights into the New Testament are not just for our own gain, of course. Most of us want to access the Greek New Testament for the sake of others, that we might teach God's Word truly, with depth of insight and with a richness of understanding. I'm not saying that you can't teach the Bible without knowing Greek. Fortunately, its story is so clear as it unfolds from Genesis to Revelation that it can be understood by a five-year-old.

But while the story is simple, it is also deep. There is always more to learn, to discover, and to enrich our understanding of who God is and what he is doing in the world. We study the Bible in depth in order to teach its story in all its richness. Greek is one tool of many that give us access to the richness of the Bible. Without it, our teaching may be sound, but it may also lack depth. In other words:

Keep your Greek for the sake of others.

I've never met a Bible teacher who wished they had not learned Greek. It's only the guys who have let it slip and no longer use it for their sermon preparation who try to tell me that Greek doesn't enhance their teaching. There's something wrong with that picture, isn't there? Of course it won't enhance your teaching if you don't use it! And if you don't use Greek, how can you really know whether it would enhance your teaching or not? It's only the people who *do* use Greek that can judge whether or not it enhances their teaching.

My own experience is that Greek *always* enhances my teaching of the Bible in some way. It may not always make a dramatic difference to my understanding of the text, though it sometimes does. But it always gives me a deeper appreciation of the text and insight into its nuances. This is the testimony of all those who have talked to me about their experiences of teaching the New Testament with a knowledge of Greek. It makes a difference.

Sometimes students ask me whether or not it is good to talk about Greek in their sermons. I usually caution against talking about it unnecessarily, though I think it is fine to do so if your hearers will really benefit. So then the inevitable question is: *If Greek doesn't make it into my sermon, then what's the point?* To which I will answer: *If you think that way, you've missed the point.* The usefulness of Greek is not so that you can tell people about what the Greek says in your sermon. The usefulness of Greek is that it will give *you* understanding of the text, which will shape what you *do* say in the sermon. It's for your preparation, and it usually remains behind the scenes. Sure, sometimes it might need to come out from behind the curtains, but generally speaking it will do its work unseen by everyone but you. But to you, the Bible teacher, Greek will make a huge difference.

How to Use This Book

While writing this book, I've occasionally caught myself sounding like one of those self-help books — *10 Steps to Instant Weight*

Loss, or something like that. I suppose that's inevitable because I am concerned to motivate you, to challenge you, and to offer you help to achieve a certain goal. But this book does not offer a guaranteed, foolproof, ten-step method to make it all happen overnight. The few self-help books I've read often leave me disappointed because they advertise themselves as being an easy, quick solution, when in actual fact they normally require lots of work and strict adherence to every rule they propose.

This book is not like that. It's not going to improve your Greek dramatically overnight, and it will take some work on your part to make it happen. Nor do I expect you to follow every suggestion I make. While I think everything here is useful, you may find one or two ideas that you won't like or don't find realistic. That's OK. Take from it what you can. Having said that, I trust you will find three or four ideas that really are necessary, such as those found in the first four chapters.

Finally, the book is better understood as sharing principles rather than "steps to success," or something like that. I suggest several different methods in the pages that follow, but you might develop your own that will work just as well, or even better. The methods you adopt are not as important as the principles behind them. However you do it, my hope is that you will develop good habits based on sound principles that will serve you well for a lifetime of reading Greek.

Chapter 1

READ EVERY DAY

Reading reminds, refreshes, and reinforces.

When the fresh seminary graduate begins pastoring, when the demands of counseling and planning meetings and checking off items on the to-do list threaten to undo you, it is more than a little difficult to sustain one's facility in Greek. Long ago I learned a trick that can help the pastor—on four or five days a week spend ten to fifteen minutes in the Greek text just reading. Open up your Greek New Testament, have a translation to its side and a lexicon to consult, use a parsing guide for words you can't parse, and just read the text itself.

One more piece of advice, and it may be the most important: *never feel guilty or stupid for what you have forgotten, and banish from your mind what your demanding seminary professors would think of what you have now forgotten.* The fast pace you used to learn Greek in seminary gives way to a decade of consistent reading and, like family love and growth in wisdom, your facility in Greek will not only develop, but you will become more and more confident that you've (only then) finally got a good handle on Greek.

Scot McKnight

Practicing Music

From my background in music, I am convinced that a little time practicing every day is much more beneficial than large chunks of practice interspersed by large chunks of inactivity. When I first started learning to play the saxophone, I found that regular practice every day sped up my development on the instrument in a way that couldn't be matched by a less regular approach. More than twenty years later, I still find this to be true. If I want to step it up a bit for an important concert or recording, or if I just want to get my saxophone playing to the next level, a little bit each day is the way.

For most musicians, that's a no-brainer. Of course it's better to practice every day. But my point is that *a little bit* of practice every day is better than longer periods at less frequent intervals. Even if you end up doing the same amount of practice in a week through either approach, a little bit each day works out better than the spread-out approach.

Why is that? Well, I'm no expert on brain development, and I don't know the neurological and physiological reasons why a daily approach is better than a more sporadic approach, but here are a few thoughts. I know that I feel *more confident* when I practice every day. Everything is that much more familiar and fresh in my mind. It's more comfortable so I'm more confident. I also think that the neurological connections that are made in the brain are reinforced and strengthened by daily practice.

Moreover, I believe that a lot of development occurs in the subconscious mind, *away* from the instrument. But this is triggered after a practice session. After I practice, my brain continues to work on improving my skills — just ticking away in the background of my subconscious mind. I suppose that sounds a bit Zen, but lots of good musicians know it to be true. Thus, by practicing a while each day, my brain is regularly triggered to keep working at developing those skills.

Reading Greek

In the same way, a little bit of reading Greek every day keeps it all ticking along. Reading every day increases your confidence. Vocabulary, grammar, and syntax all feel more familiar with everyday exposure. Your subconscious mind is triggered regularly to reinforce your learning and knowledge.

It's *reading* Greek every day that really counts, rather than other (often good) habits. Learning Greek vocabulary, practicing paradigms, and other such things have their place, and I'll discuss them later in this book. But they are no substitute for *reading* Greek, and for busy people who can only afford to do one thing related to Greek each day, it must be this.

There are several reasons for this.

First, reading Greek is our goal. It's why we've learned Greek in the first place: to read and understand the Greek New Testament. There's nothing like practicing to achieve your goal.

Second, reading Greek brings all the other skills into play: vocabulary, grammar, and syntax are all required for reading, and the reading reminds, refreshes, and reinforces all those things.

Third, there is no substitute for getting the *vibe* of Greek besides reading it. As with all languages, there is an X-factor to Greek—a vibe, an inner coherence—that is impossible to catch without reading a lot of Greek. Verb tables alone won't do it. Vocab alone won't do it. Reading grammars and monographs about Greek won't do it either. Only reading actual Greek text will do it. It is far and away the most important thing to be doing in order to keep your Greek, and indeed to advance your Greek.

And it only has to be a small amount of reading. Half an hour reading Greek each day would be terrific, but even ten minutes is great. I know some guys who just aim to read one sentence of Greek a day. It doesn't have to involve a big-time commitment— just do a little each day. You'd be surprised at how much difference ten minutes of reading Greek each day makes over the long term. It doesn't feel like much at the time, but it will do wonders for your knowledge and ability. So, don't despise "the day of small things"; a little bit is what you want. A little bit is the key.

In fact, I would recommend starting smaller rather than bigger, especially if your Greek is rusty. Half an hour of reading Greek could do you more damage than good to begin with because the confidence factor is really important here. If you read for half an hour and end up deeply discouraged, or if you despair at how much you don't know, you'll be less likely to stay the course. Start small. Read for ten minutes a day and don't worry about how much you don't know or how little text you cover in that time. You will gradually find yourself wanting to read for longer. If you have the time in the day to increase to fifteen or twenty minutes, or eventually thirty minutes, that's great. Just don't bite off more than you can chew to begin with.

Here's another tip: begin with "easy" Greek, like John's gospel. The vocabulary is limited and the syntax is straightforward (while the theology is profound!). This will help your confidence and get you into the swing of things. If you've been away from Greek for quite a while, starting off with 1 Peter or Hebrews would be a big mistake. Even Paul might be too much for now. That's OK; we'll get there in time.

Your Habit

The key here is to develop a habit. As with all good habits, it may take some motivation and energy to get started. But once the pattern is established and you are reading some Greek each day, the habit will take care of itself. It will become as routine as brushing your teeth.

It's worth noting, too, however, that reading every day need not become a type of legalism that leaves you feeling guilty or inadequate if you miss a day here or there. It's OK to miss an occasional day during a particularly busy time. In fact, you may decide you want to read five days a week and take weekends off. That's perfectly fine. The important thing is that a habit is formed in which you are reading some Greek at least several times a week. If you can develop this habit, you will be well on your way to keeping your Greek.

Summary: Reading Greek is not only effective for maintaining and developing your Greek skills; it can also be done regularly without a huge time commitment.

Blog Responses

Shane Thanks Con. Helpful hint, though I sometimes feel I never really learnt Greek well enough in the first place to keep it up — I just satisfied my examiners then moved on, with the odd reference to the language every now and then. What would you recommend for the person who needs serious review?

Con Campbell Thanks, Shane, that's an important issue, and I think I'll address it in a future post. Stay tuned!

Mark Stevens Thank you for this very encouraging post. As a minister with little spare time to spend hours reviewing it is nice to know my "little bit" every day helps. I personally try to read a bit in my morning Bible reading. I would be interested to know what you think of using software such as Logos to help the process of reading Greek.

Gazman Hey, Con, my problem is that the first thing that has gone from my grey matter is the vocab, especially reading books we didn't cover at College (and even those we did, to be honest).

This is one of my problems with trying to read every day, apart from my random nature that despises routine. I try and structurally chart the flow of each passage I preach on, as verb forms, prepositions, clause markers, etc. are still easily recognisable. Then I can just look up the words I don't recognise much more easily (although preparing a series on 2 Peter has got my brain to bursting point). Do you reckon this might be helpful for others as well?

Con Campbell Hi Gazman, thanks for your comments. I'll address the issue of vocab down the track, but I think flowcharting is enormously helpful in its own right, and I think if it helps you to keep your Greek ticking over, then all the better.

Mark, I'll comment about software soon ... (promises, promises).

Laura "A little bit every day keeps it all ticking along. And it really only has to be a little. Half an hour reading Greek each day would be terrific, but even ten minutes would be great." ... Hence the Greek NT in my parents' bathroom at home.

Con Campbell lol!

Wayne Connor Thanks Con. Would a word a day work?

Chapter 2

BURN YOUR INTERLINEAR

The interlinear is a tool of the devil, designed to make preachers stupid.

> One of the great joys of Christian ministry is to be able to open the Greek New Testament and prepare your sermon from what was written. It is a privilege that few people in our busy world have—to be set aside from other tasks to read the Bible carefully in order to preach God's Word faithfully to others. Few disciplines bring greater reward than the careful comprehension of the text of Scripture, and it must not be left to translators or academics but be found in the pastoral leadership of the church.
>
> *Phillip D. Jensen*

A tool of the devil? I'm kidding, of course—interlinears have their place. If you don't know much Greek, and have no intention of getting good at it, then an interlinear can be useful to check a word here or there and see what Greek word underlies an English translation. But if you want to keep your Greek, if you want to develop your Greek, if you want to read the Greek New Testament, then take your interlinear outside, douse it with gasoline, and light a match.

Does that sound harsh? Let me explain why I think this way.

In the Gym

When I'm exercising with weights in the gym, there's often a temptation to cheat. Some weight-lifting exercises isolate certain muscle groups so that you can really work out the part of the body that you want to train. One obvious example is the bicep curl. As you raise the dumbbell from a straight arm position toward your shoulder, bending at the elbow, your bicep is targeted and does most of the work. The trouble I have with the bicep curl, however, is that as my bicep gets tired, it's really easy to cheat. If you *swing* the weight up to your shoulder, you let momentum lift the weight and take the pressure off the bicep. Or if you flare your elbow out to the side instead of keeping it close to your body, your shoulder will pick up the strain, again letting the bicep off the hook. That's what I mean by "cheating" in the gym.

Well, what's wrong with that? If the bicep is really hurting and I just *can't* lift the weight anymore using the bicep, what harm is there in getting some help from other muscles? At least I'm still doing the bicep curl, right? I'll finish off the set and feel good about it, rather than not complete the set. Surely, completion is better than failure, right?

Wrong!

First of all, weights do you no good if your muscles don't hurt. Hurting them is the idea! Muscle strength develops by tearing muscle fibres in the gym and by your body rebuilding the muscle in the week that follows. But if you don't *really* work that muscle and really tear those fibres, your body will have less to do in rebuilding the muscle; as a result your muscle will not get much stronger. *It has to hurt.*

Second, if you "cheat" in the gym, you may not work the muscle you're aiming for at all. Who cares whether you finish the set if the muscle you're training doesn't get worked out? There's no point in that. The other muscles that help you to cheat are just a crutch to support the weaker muscle, but it's the weaker muscle that really needs to be challenged. Otherwise it will stay weak, because your stronger muscles will continue to do the work. Cheating with a crutch promotes weakness.

What's the real issue here? I find that it's the *inner struggle* at the gym that needs to be worked through properly. If I cheat, I might feel good about finishing the set, even though the exercise will not be truly effective. Or I can do the exercise properly, but risk not completing the set—and risk failure. So I'm faced with a decision. Do I want to feel good about myself, or do I want to do the job I came to do? At the gym, I need to be honest about where I'm really at. Pretending to be stronger than I am promotes weakness.

The Interlinear

An interlinear is like a crutch. Instead of relying on the Greek you know, an interlinear props you up and helps you to finish "the set." Instead of using the primary "muscle group" needed to read Greek—your memory!—the interlinear allows you to underwork your memory and rely on the stronger "muscle group"—the printed English vocabulary sitting right there under each Greek word.

An interlinear helps you to avoid pain, just like cheating in the gym. It can be frustrating not to know what the Greek words mean; it feels slow and tedious; and perhaps worst of all, it can be painful to face up to the fact that your Greek is weaker than you'd like. But—just like training in the gym—we need to face up to our weakness if we're going to get any stronger. If you pretend to be strong when you're not, you'll keep compensating for your weakness through other means, and you won't make any progress. If you don't have the patience to work through the pain and frustration of being slow or inadequate in reading Greek, you won't get any better. The quick way out will always win. And when the quick way wins, so does weakness.

You need to decide. Will you be honest and face up to the (possibly painful) truth about how good your Greek really is? Or would you rather feel good about yourself—pretending to read Greek, denying reality—and just go on "cheating"? Your answer to that question will determine whether you will keep developing your Greek in the long term. As they say, no pain, no gain.

The real problem with an interlinear is that it shortcuts the learning process. Since an English word is right there under each Greek word, you really don't stand a chance. The English translation is *right there*! How can you *not* look at it? Even if you try not to, your peripheral vision is going to take in what's there.

Of course, if you don't know some of the words, you'll need some help, and we'll come to the topic of vocabulary aids—and improving your vocabulary—in a later chapter. When you use an interlinear, however, your brain won't even get a chance to work out whether or not it knows a word. That's right, you won't even *know* if you know the Greek! Before giving your brain the opportunity to register what's happening with the Greek, your eyes betray you as you look at the English gloss.

Moreover, with an interlinear, you won't struggle to make sense of the Greek sentence. Not only will it shortcut your ability to remember vocabulary, but the interlinear will deaden your ability to understand Greek syntax. Instead of struggling with Greek word order, with what the subject, object, and indirect object are in the sentence, and with how the clauses relate to each other, you'll default to the English vocabulary and work out how to order the words based on what you can piece together from the English (or based on your memory of having read that passage in English months earlier).

All in all, to those who want to keep their Greek, improve their Greek, and read Greek at all, the interlinear is not helpful. It will not promote your Greek ability. In fact, it will weaken your Greek. Just as bicep curls without straining your biceps is counterproductive, so too is reading Greek without really using your Greek. Remember: with an interlinear, you won't practice your Greek—and without practice, your Greek will slowly die.

So, go ahead and burn that interlinear. Or, at least, give it to someone you don't like very much.

Summary: Reading Greek = good. Interlinear = bad. Bicep curls = ouch!

Blog Responses

Stanley Yea — I gave away my interlinear. I'm really grateful that I did too!

John You're not going to hammer the *Reader's Greek New Testament*, are you, Con? Seriously, there are some words that none of us could be bothered to learn. (None of us except you, of course!)

Gordon Cheng Loving your blog, Con.

Lose the interlinear? Ooh, that's cruel. I love mine like an uncoordinated kid loves his training wheels, or at least I did until I got Accordance and now I just flick my eyes from side-to-side and do the best I can.

There was that time in NT with David Peterson when I tried to translate aloud while reading slowly and haltingly from the NASB, but my fellow students sprung me. Had it been high school rather than Moore College, I would have copped a detention.

I actually found my interlinear kept me reading Greek when it was all getting too hard and depressing. Like with music — you naturals just get up and do it, we poor old plods sit at home with our metronomes ticking. But at least we're still having a go.

Con Campbell Thanks for sharing, Gordon. I would never have described you as a "poor old plod," but that NT story is hilarious.

David McKay If you want to learn to play the piano, writing the names of the white notes on them will slow you down, not help you remember the note names. Similarly, writing the names of the notes under the printed score makes it harder, not easier to read the music.

Con Campbell Good one, David!

Dan Anderson Perhaps you could subtitle your book, "What would Hercules do?"

Con Campbell Dan, I think "What would Arnold do?" would be more like it . . .

Matoke Thanks a lot for this stern warning. It is easy to think that the more you use these other tools, the better you'll get with Greek.

Jason Chamberlain I often tell people that learning a biblical language is no different from learning an instrument or learning how to play a sport. There is a long learning curve to basic proficiency. The only way to develop and maintain that proficiency is through consistent and thoughtful practice. This is why I keep doing flashcards regularly and why I read at least a paragraph in my *Reader's Greek* every day.

I also have found that more exposure to the language has helped me when I use my UBS4.

Of course there are some words I don't know, but I can often figure them out by context or by breaking the word down into components.

I usually run 5k 3 times/week and 10k once/week. There are times when I can't do that because of sickness, travel, weather, etc. What I've found is that consistency breeds more consistency and better performance, but any time I have to take a break, it becomes more difficult to get back into it. Greek has been no different for me.

Chapter 3

USE SOFTWARE TOOLS WISELY

Bible software can be a blessing or a curse—it's up to you.

Quite possibly, the most significant value of knowing the biblical languages is intangible in character. Most of us are conditioned to think that nothing is truly valuable that does not have an immediate and concrete payoff, yet most of the teaching that we have received from birth is of a different nature altogether. We are simply not conscious of how deeply we have been molded by countless experiences that affect our perspective, our thinking, and our decisions. Similarly, a measure of proficiency in the biblical languages provides the framework that promotes responsibility in the handling of the biblical text. Continued exposure to the original text expands our horizon and furnishes us with a fresh and more authentic perspective than that which we bring from our modern, English-speaking situation.

Moisés Silva

Software tools, such as Accordance, Logos, and BibleWorks, are amazing, and they can be used for great good. They are enormously powerful tools for searching the Bible and for doing research. My doctorate would have taken ten years without the aid of BibleWorks. When it comes to reading Greek, the instantaneous help that software offers can make the whole process less frustrating and time consuming, especially when you need help with vocabulary. To have immediate access to lexical information and parsing can be genuinely useful.

But like many good things, Bible software can be abused, with terrible consequences.

Driving a Car

Where I live, in Newtown, Sydney, I don't often need to use a car. I walk most places, or occasionally catch a bus. But when I *do* need to use the car (because public transport will not take me where I need to go, or because it would take too long; but don't get me started about Sydney public transport . . .), I would be lost without it. I'm entirely used to having the convenience of getting around in a car when I need to, and life without one — for me — would be a real hassle at times.

Of course, people have survived just fine without cars for thousands of years, and even now many people do not drive. So, cars are not *essential*, right? Of course not. But once you get used to the speed and convenience of getting where you need to go by driving, it's hard to go back. The same goes for public transport — what if there were no buses, trains, or planes? We'd be left with walking, horses, and camels — which may suit some people, but not me!

But as useful as cars are — and as time-efficient as they may be — they can also be dangerous. Hundreds of people die every year through car-related incidents. But does that mean we shouldn't drive? For most of us, it means that we will drive, but take great care in doing so, knowing how dangerous it can be. And why are cars dangerous? Because of their speed, of course. In

other words, the very thing that makes them effective for trans-
portation is also the thing that may threaten life.

As they say in my neck of the woods, speed kills.

My kids are not old enough to drive yet (and won't be for a
loooong time, I might add), but when they get to that age, I'll
want them to learn to drive. But I will worry about their safety
too. I'll warn them about the dangers of speed and the importance
of not abusing it. I'll teach them to be self-controlled and careful
with the machine that will afford them great convenience, but at
some risk.

Bible Software

You probably get where this is going. Bible software tools provide
incredible speed and convenience, and they offer such a significant boost in this way that it would be crazy not to harness that
power. But, they come at a risk. And — just like cars — the very
thing that makes them convenient is also the thing that threatens
to kill your Greek. Speed. You can look up what a Greek word
means with a small move of the mouse. You can consult a translation with no effort at all. You can parse Greek words faster than
you can say *paradigm*. But how does the speed of a software tool
kill?

In much the same way that an interlinear can be a crutch and
shortcut the learning process, so software tools can be used such
that your Greek will suffer — and possibly die. By moving that
cursor too quickly, you can replicate the perennial problem that
is inflicted by the dreaded interlinear (which you have recently
burnt). Remember that the main problem with the interlinear is
that you see the English words underneath the Greek words and
therefore don't give your brain a chance to work its Greek magic.
In fact — as I pointed out in the last chapter — you don't even get
the chance to work out *if* you know the Greek words before the
wretched English gloss makes your Greek weak. Well, software

will be no different from an interlinear in its negative effects if you are too quick to look up the answers.

So, my advice to you is the same as it will be to my kids when they're old enough to drive (remember: in the *way*-distant future): by all means harness the power of software tools, but be careful that their speed does not kill your Greek.

Here are some tips for using software in order to keep — rather than kill — your Greek.

1. When you are doing your ten to thirty minutes per day of Greek reading (see chapter 1), do not have an English translation open on the screen. Make sure you can see only the Greek (all the software programs enable this). Feel free to check an English translation once you've done some reading (perhaps after each verse, or after a paragraph), but don't look at it while you're trying to read the Greek. In this way, you'll be replicating the experience of reading a (paper) Greek New Testament, though the advantages of the software are still close to hand.

When I use Accordance for my Greek reading, I use its tabs to good effect. One tab is for Greek — and only Greek is open in that tab — and another tab is for an English translation of the same passage. In fact, if you read other languages too, you can have a tab for each if you wish. When I read Greek, I'll read a paragraph or so without any reference to an English translation. Then, when I think I've worked out the best way to handle the Greek, I'll take a look at a translation and see how it compares. I'm not so much looking to see if I was "right," but how the translators decided to handle the passage. Of course, a translation can be useful to "correct" your reading too, if you realize that you have misunderstood or misread something in the Greek passage.

2. Be slow to move that cursor. Or turn off the "instant details" function of the program. The risk of using software is that you can shortcut the learning process, just as you will with an interlinear. You need to struggle to remember words and grammar rather

than just get a quick answer. (By the way, this need only apply to your "Greek reading time," not necessarily every time you use the software.) It's really important to give yourself a chance to work at the Greek before getting help. I know it will slow things down, and it might be a little frustrating, but holding off even just for a few seconds could make all the difference in the long term.

Sometimes I find that if there's a word that I don't remember right away, it will come to me if I give it a little more time. Or I'll make myself reach for the mnemonic that I worked out for the word when I originally learned it (more on mnemonics later). And if that works, then my memory of that word will be significantly reinforced. But if I lose patience and go straight for the "instant details," my connection to that word will be weakened rather than strengthened.

3. A problem with software is that it doesn't tell you (by default) which words you should already know. You think you don't know a word, so you get the quick answer; then you think, "Oh yeah, I knew that." That's not a good outcome. Even if you think you're learning that way, because you've reviewed a word that you'd forgotten, it's not actually the case. If you think, "I knew that," you've missed an opportunity to strengthen that knowledge and instead practiced a shortcut. And it's shortcuts that will really weaken your vocab.

Having said that, the blog comments below suggest ways that this problem may be circumvented on the various software tools. Check it out. Another option is to use a vocabulary tool like Burer and Miller's book, which will conveniently list rare words for each chapter in the New Testament. But we'll address vocab review and learning more fully in the next chapter.

Summary: If you're disciplined, go ahead and use software for your Greek reading. But if you can't be trusted not to cheat, then close your laptop and get out a paper Greek New Testament. If you can find one.

Blog Responses

Stanley So Con, would a Greek reader be helpful?

Con Campbell Don't worry, Stan, I'll get to Greek readers ...

Stanley D'OH! Just from that comment, I'm thinking you're erring on the **bad** side of Greek readers rather than good ...

Con Campbell You'll have to wait and see!

Dave Miers Fingers are crossed that Greek readers are okay. For the record ... Stan encouraged me to get a Greek reader. Enjoying this series — thanks Con.

Mike Aubrey Thanks, Con, these have been good tips thus far. Keep it up!

Laura Couldn't agree more about not resorting to the English too quickly. When my Greek was at its best (ugh, ages ago), it was when I was actually doing parts of my devotional reading in my GNT. I'd get stuck on a word, work through it grammatically, have a think about context, and THEN pull up the English (or, more likely, just look up the word in the back ...) to bail me out if I still needed it. That was a time when Greek was a total joy for me.

This series is inspiring me to get back at it. I'm teaching Latin for the first time this year, so that refresher in language and grammar might be just what my brain needs to be able to process it all again. Thanks!

Con Campbell Thanks for your comments, guys.

Rick Bennett Hi Con, good post. I just wrote a follow-up post at Accordance (www.accordancebible.com/3314718) showing a couple tips on how users can responsibly use our software to keep up with their Greek, along with my own version of a Greek Reader. I tried to specifically address your request on how it is possible to indicate in the text which words someone should know based on their frequency. I look forward to your future installments.

Best,
Rick, Accordance Development Team

Con Campbell Thanks, Rick, that is a very helpful post.

Dan Cole G'day Con, thanks for the posts! It is also possible to graphically indicate the vocab that has not been learned in BibleWorks7 (and I assume in BW8) using an inclusion/exclusion list (IEL). Although the process seems slightly more involved than Accordance, it's not hard to get the hang of. Also, because the list of words is saved in an IEL file, you can use the word list manager to modify the list of unknown words by both frequency and passage, as well as manually. This means that as further vocab is learned, it can be easily removed from the list and text formatting can then be adjusted to reflect this.

Con Campbell Thanks Dan, that is also helpful.

Mark Stevens Thanks Con, you were a lot more gracious than I thought you might be. As a minister with limited time and a desire to begin with original languages when it comes to sermon prep, software (such as Logos Original Languages) is a godsend. The reminder to do some "daily" Greek to keep the learning active is a good counter to the daily use of software. I would say that Bible study software that is language proficient is a must for all ministers. It amazes me how many ministers let go of their language skills when they could so easily keep it up with sermon prep alone. Once again, cheers!

Ben Hudson Hey Con, I sometimes use a search like this: [Range John 1:1 – 18] [Count 1 – 30] in Accordance so that the words I should know (i.e., vocab occurring more than 30 times in the NT) show up in black and the words I can "cursor" are in red. N.B. — you often have to add a few verses of "context" so that all the verses show up.

Con Campbell Thanks, Ben.

Redpooba Perhaps knowing paradigms like a parrot should not be our goal, for obviously even a parrot could do this. Our goal is rather to know God's Word. But there is no replacement for what Dr. Campbell is calling for, interacting with the Greek (i.e., the Word) on a consistent basis so that it becomes more and more internalized. And this only comes from having seen it again and again, not like a parrot but like a child learns. So also we must interact with the languages consistently, even if in small bites, to ever hope to really understand more than a few facts about what form the words are in.

Dr. Campbell is completely correct to point out that wrong learning methods serve to have big biceps without the ability to walk over to the object which we wish to pick up. Thanks for the posts, solid and practical reflections. Professor Campbell, are you going to make mention of the benefits of reading out loud or other audio methods being mixed with the visual?

Chris Thomas I think that using the Greek is the best way to prevent losing it. The first thing to do is translate sentences every day/week. Just doing ten sentences a week like one did in school (I learned Greek at a secular university) can go a long way to keeping it sharp. Just as a sword needs to be sharpened, so too does honing one's Greek need a little work. If the work is done consistently, then one does not need to spend a long time doing it. However, a blade that has become dull due to sitting around for a long time takes longer to put an edge back on.

The second thing I would suggest is to teach Greek. I teach Greek on a volunteer basis. It is only an introductory class, but I find that it helps the body of Christ and also helps me maintain my skills.

Mark Vitalis Hoffman I agree with both Redpooba and Chris Thomas, but I spent 14 years in parish ministry before becoming a seminary teacher. I was pretty adept at Greek, but it really suffered in the parish. As much as I love reading and studying the Greek, if someone is in the hospital, that had to be my priority. Teaching confirmation classes and preparing sermons gave me the excuse to look at the texts, but most of the time I had to move rather quickly from the texts to getting something ready to go.

Exotesparemboles Bible software tools are like credits cards: they are not bad in and of themselves. They can be helpful when used wisely, but they can quickly become harmful when one becomes dependent on and indebted to them.

Bill Mazey Years ago I took two years of Greek at Cedarville College under the great teaching of Dr. Robert Gromacki. I remember him encouraging us to look for the prepositional phrases in our translation work. I can't say that I was his best student, but I still try to keep up with my Greek studies. I keep a copy of the Greek NT and Machen's *New Testament Greek for Beginners* in my briefcase. I try to keep going over the fundamentals.

I remember Dr. Gromacki as a man of prayer. He encouraged us to pray and ask God to help us learn Greek as we studied it. While taking his class I found the following quote and wrote in the front of my Greek NT: "After all is said and done, the only way to know the Greek Testament properly is by prayer." — J. B. Lightfoot.

Con Campbell Thanks for the Lightfoot quote. What a champ!

Chapter 4

MAKE VOCABULARY YOUR FRIEND

You remember the names
of your friends, right?

Are you old enough to remember the song that begins, "It only takes a spark to get a fire going"? Well, sometimes it only takes a (Greek) word to get a sermon going. A few years ago as I was thinking about an upcoming Advent message, I decided to read Luke 2 one more time in Greek to see if I had missed anything. It's tough after a few years in the pulpit not to have every sermon in the Christmas season sound about the same. When I did so, I came across the Greek word στρατία, usually translated "host" (a.k.a. "choir"), in Luke 2:13. That word, which occurs only twice in the New Testament, ended up sending me on a journey of several years. It led first to a message with fresh insights on the scene of the shepherds in Bethlehem, and then to a paper delivered at the annual Evangelical Theological Society convention, to an article published in the *Calvin Theological Journal*, and even to an entire book with new thoughts for reflection on the Christmas story. Pay attention to words.

Verlyn D. Verbrugge

Clearly one of the hardest elements of keeping your Greek is vocabulary. Even if you remember your paradigms and recall the syntax, without knowing what the words *mean*, it is all for nought! Not only is vocabulary easily forgotten, there are many words that only appear once or twice in the New Testament. All of this means that vocabulary acquisition and retention can become a major hurdle for keeping your Greek.

I get the impression that some people are "above" learning vocabulary. What I mean is that vocab learning is not especially sexy or sophisticated, like, say, verbal aspect ☺. It doesn't necessarily tax your intellect or feel like you are reaching into the deep mysteries at the heart of this exotic language. For most people — even most Greek geeks — vocabulary learning is a chore. That may be why there are guys who know their verb paradigms back to front, but still struggle to read a Greek sentence. They can tell me that the verb in front of them is an aorist passive indicative, third person plural. They can tell me that the aorist encodes perfective aspect, which conveys a summary viewpoint of the action. But that doesn't help much if they don't know what the action *is*. This is the reality of things, people. The hardest thing to master in Greek (apart from, perhaps, the rules of accentuation) is the vocabulary. Learn the vocab, and you'll be able to read Greek. It's that simple.

But even if you're convinced of the importance of knowing Greek vocabulary, it is still hard work for most people. It's worth thinking through a few different ways to tackle this. For one thing, I suggest that there are two different "modes" of vocab study. The first is the mode that the student is in when he or she is first learning Greek, and is literally seeing most Greek words for the first time. The second is the mode that someone is in after they've studied Greek intensely and just wants to maintain their skills, or perhaps gradually improve over time.

For those in the first "mode," my main suggestion is to make your first contact with a word really count. While it can be tempting to rush your vocab learning—since there are so many words to master—it's important to let quality rule over quantity. So, for example, when you learn a new word, don't just let your short-term memory do the work. Some people might be able to look at a list of ten new words and remember most (if not all) of them without any trouble. Such people might be tempted to think that remembering words without much effort is doing the job you need to do, but often it isn't.

When I was first learning Greek, I found that the words that I just "trusted myself" to remember did not stick as well as the words that I really took my time with. When I was patient enough to think of a memory hook (I'll talk more about these below) for each new word, I found that these words really did stick, and for many of these I still remember the original hook. These words did not require the same level of review in the future, and I retain that vocab without any trouble. Take your time with it, and you'll save time and frustration later.

For those in the second "mode," my suggestion is similar in that you should take your time with words that are familiar but do not come to you right away. It's better for your memory to pause and think on the word, rather than to decide impatiently that you don't remember the word and look it up. The words that you recall slowly are the ones that really need work, and the simple practice of waiting for yourself to remember such words is sometimes all they need to be cemented in your mind. If you look up these "slow recall" words too quickly, you'll miss the opportunity to strengthen your ability.

The following tips are in two groups. The first group is about how to learn words, and it relates to the memory and the actual skill of vocab mastery. The second group offers some practical tips about using tools to do this.

How to Learn Words

1. Invent a memory hook for each word. Some people do this intuitively, and it's not a particularly novel approach, but trust

me, it really works! Most memory techniques that involve rapid mastery of new material involve mnemonics or memory hooks in some form. Most of the time, I find that a good hook has a logic to it that will lead me from the Greek word to the gloss I wish to remember for that word. This is sometimes onomatopoeic. That is, the *sound* of the Greek word will make me think of something that I can use to remember its meaning, like πίνω, *to drink*, which makes me think of *pinot noir*. Often an English cognate will provide an obvious link to the meaning of a Greek word, like ἄγγελος, *angel*. Both of these types of hooks are the easy ones. Other times, we need to get more creative. For example, the hook I use for χείρ, *hand*, is: "As a saxophonist, I need to take 'care' of my *hands*."

The great thing about a good memory hook is that it will really help to keep the word in your long-term memory, because the connection that's made makes a lasting impression in your mind. There are many words that I learned ten years ago for which I not only remember the hook I used to learn them, but I remember where I was when I came up with the hook.

2. Make each word your friend. This idea comes from music and, in particular, from my former saxophone teacher, Harold Luebke. His advice to me about learning scales was that each scale needs to become a "friend." What he meant by that was that I should know each scale so well that no scale would feel difficult or uncomfortable. And I knew right away what he meant by that. The scales that I found "easy" were the ones that I knew really well. They were not threatening; in fact, they were *fun* to play!

That advice really helped me with my scales on the saxophone, and from my first year of learning Greek, I endeavoured to adopt the same mind-set (and it can be applied to paradigms as well as vocab). Upon reflection, I suppose that this advice is not so much a technique for learning vocabulary as it is a goal. Creating memory hooks is a technique, but it's useful to have a goal that the technique helps to achieve.

3. Pronounce each word. This is especially important for aural learners, but everyone should do it. The more that other senses can be utilized, the more likely it is that your memory will latch on to a word. While it's unlikely that you'll be able to utilize your sense of smell and touch, at least hearing can be effective. What's more, it's good for your Greek pronunciation to practice saying words out loud (even if it's under your breath).

4. Listen to vocab. Some people like to record their Greek vocab and listen to it in the car, on the iPod, or whatever. Audio vocab tools can also be purchased for download from Zondervan. Obviously, this is a good one for aural learners, but it can help others too, since the more senses that are involved in learning, the better.

5. For those with the inclination, you can try writing out vocabulary. The manual process of spelling words out on paper helps to make them stick for some people, especially kinesthetic learners. It might also help you to increase your familiarity with words, since you'll see them in your own handwriting. This one is not so great for me, since I can rarely read my own handwriting!

6. Again, for those so inclined, you can try practicing going from English to Greek. Most software vocab tools allow this option. I would describe this as a more advanced technique — certainly not necessary or realistic for the majority of people — but if you're looking for something to stretch you further and to really consolidate your vocab, this may be what you're looking for. The reason it works is that you really have to know your vocab to produce the Greek from the English. And even if this is a struggle for you, after some practice going from English to Greek, you should find that Greek to English becomes a lot easier!

7. Make vocab a part of your life. Vocabulary learning and retention needs to be a long-term pursuit. But the reality is that it will drop off the radar for most busy people unless you develop a pattern or habit that does not take too much time or effort. This will be different for different people, and we each need to think about how to do this for ourselves. I use my iPhone to do this in

a way that is fun and makes use of time in my day that might otherwise be wasted (more on this below).

Tools

1. I've already mentioned the risks of using software to help with vocabulary, though there are ways to resolve these issues. A favourite tool of mine, however, is Burer and Miller's *A New Reader's Lexicon of the Greek New Testament*. You need to learn all the vocabulary that occurs more than fifty times in the New Testament (most first-year Greek students will achieve that, and I recommend learning all words above twenty times), and then the vocabulary that occurs less than fifty times is listed for each chapter in which the words appear. This means that you can open any chapter of the New Testament, open *NRL* to the same chapter, and have all the vocabulary you need at your fingertips. Using this tool, you can know immediately whether you should already know a word or not, and those you don't know are there for you to see.

2. You can use *NRL* to acquire new vocabulary in a fun way. Before you read a particular passage, look up the section in *NRL* that addresses that passage, and go through all the vocabulary that you don't know. If you give yourself enough time, you can learn these words; it will only be a few if you are going to read Greek for ten minutes or so. Then when you read the passage, you will know all its vocabulary. You will enjoy reading Greek like never before, since you will not need to look anything up. This is especially useful if you're preaching on a passage at the end of the week. If you're working with one passage all week, you can become really familiar with its vocabulary. So, you can use *NRL* to strengthen your vocab and speed up sermon preparation!

3. *A Reader's Greek New Testament* is a good tool. Yup, I am finally getting to this book. Only the rarer vocab words (thirty times and below) are provided, and they're at the bottom of the

page—rather than, like interlinears, alongside the Greek. This will basically achieve the same thing as *NRL* when seeking help with rare vocabulary. One possible drawback is that it might be more difficult to learn new vocab ahead of time, the way you can with *NRL*. But if it works for you to do that, then great.

Another possible drawback is that you will probably never learn the rarer words, because they are always there on the page. With *NRL*, you can put it away after learning new words, so it doesn't shortcut the learning process. But then, you're probably thinking, "Who cares about the rare words, except geeks like you?" Point taken!

Summary: By making words your friends, you will take a lot of the frustration out of reading Greek, and instead you'll enjoy more quality time with buddies!

Blog Responses

Jthom18 In terms of vocabulary, some of the Zondervan materials have been placed on Audible for download. This is helpful for anyone whose digital player goes everywhere with them like mine does. The *Readings in the Greek New Testament* and *New Testament Greek Vocabulary: Learn on the Go* can be helpful in keeping the vocabulary in mind while driving or exercising. There is an ad for a trial that would let someone get some of the Greek resources for free.

Con Campbell Thanks for those references.

Dave Miers Glad the Greek reader wasn't trashed!!

Alex Kowalenko I purchased the *Reader's Greek New Testament* last year, and I really like it. It is great for traveling, or for church as you only need to take with you one book, instead of 2 (or 3 including an English Bible — but who only takes 2 books with them when traveling!).

Lionel Windsor Hi Con — I agree entirely. Vocab learning may initially be the most plodding, boring part of learning Greek — but the more vocab you know, the more you'll love reading the Greek text itself, because you'll keep recognising the smiling faces of your "friends" popping up all over the place. Since motivation is one of the biggest factors in learning a language, learning vocab is one of the primary ways to ramp up your motivation.

Con Campbell Thanks, Lionel. Motivation is a really important factor, for sure.

Carl Conrad I made a practice in grad school of noting down on a list words that I either didn't recognize or couldn't guess at from context and then studying the lexical entries for words that recurred on my list. I think that successful vocabulary acquisition depends upon some real study of lexical entries and getting a feel for the contexts in which particular words are used.

Con Campbell Thanks for that point, Carl. Doing some actual lexical work on vocabulary in order to learn the words is an interesting idea.

Jason Chamberlain I maintain that a day without flashcards is like a day without sunshine. There is absolutely no substitute for regular, methodical review. I've been done with my Greek classes for about

18 months, but still review my vocabulary daily using software called Anki. I don't do as much as I did when I was reviewing for weekly vocab quizzes, but I also realize that if I don't review I'm going to forget. I'm also trying to slowly make progress on new words so that I can get my vocab down to around 10 occurrences.

Exotesparemboles Just as there are two sides to a coin, so are there two sides to a flashcard! Try working through your flashcards by going from Greek to English, and then when you are finished working through the stack, flip the stack over and work through your cards by going from English to Greek!

Another idea to really learn by going from English to Greek is to work through your flashcards by reading the English word on the flashcard, and then actually writing out the Greek word on a separate piece of paper.

Con Campbell Interesting idea, thanks!

Laura "The great thing about a good memory hook is that it will really help to keep the word in your long-term memory, because the connection that's made makes a lasting impression in your mind."

Even a BAD memory hook makes a lasting impression. I remember the ridiculous, thin-stretched mnemonic devices I used when learning Greek vocab in college, and despite the fact that I would NEVER recommend 90% of them to others, they still stick with me. I think my preposition mnemonics were the worst, and the most effective.

I'm taking a couple of my students through Mounce this year and I tell them to use any hook they can think of — the sillier and weirder the better.

Con Campbell Nice one! Though I would call those GOOD memory hooks, not bad ones; if they work, they're good!

David Blackburn Your post reminded me of my seminary days. Memorising Greek and Hebrew vocab was hard mental work but there were rewards. Translation and diagramming became easier. This helped with exegetical and homiletical outlining. In fact, after many years in the ministry, I still experience the rewards of memorising Greek in my preaching preparation.

Jason Chamberlain I have found memory hooks to be very useful. I still remember a classmate mentioning "no stew" for νηστεύω ("I fast") to help remember its meaning. However, I come up with hooks for words that I find confusing because there is another word that looks or sounds similar. I don't take the time to do it for each word.

I do pronounce each word in my head as I go through flashcards. I'm normally in a setting where saying each word out loud would get me some funny looks.

Scott D. Andersen As I read the GNT, I had thought that if I write an occasional verse that especially jumps out at me (either for devotional reasons, grammatical reasons or vocab enhancement) in my Moleskine and then make that verse a Greek memory verse, my grasp of the vocab and grammar would increase by means of the compiled databank within my own memory. Does that make sense? I'm hoping that just as hiding the Word itself in my heart is useful for increasing understanding, teaching, and theology, so also would hiding God's Word in Greek in my heart be useful for these.

Con Campbell Greek memory verses are an interesting idea! Probably for more advanced users, I would say.

Laura Tooootally stealing this idea for my Greek students.

Rusty Osborne I heartily agree with the methods prescribed above, and I have benefitted from all of them in learning vocabulary. My newest strategy for keeping and gradually advancing my Greek vocabulary is to make frequency-based vocab lists using Accordance. For example, I am currently reading 1 Peter along with Clowney's commentary, and I have made a vocab list of the words used in 1 Peter 20x or less (kind of like Kubo's "special vocab"). I try to be diligent enough to learn the vocab for the verses that I will read following the commentary's divisions — typically 5–10 verses. So far, I have been pleased with the results. I have found that studying the vocab and then seeing it contextually in my reading helps me remember it. Hope this helps.

Con Campbell Gold! Thanks.

Laura I do this with my Latin students, and I'm thinking of assigning it for my Greek students too — if there is an English derivative (obviously much more common with Latin), they write it on the

back of their vocab card above the definition
and they're responsible for memorizing at least
one derivative for each vocabulary word. Some
derivatives are obvious (especially the preposi-
tion-based ones), but I find it quite helpful to be
deliberate in learning derivatives, even if they're
really obscure or arcane, and even if they're not
English words you're immediately familiar with.
It just creates another memory hook — a neural
pathway, so to speak.

Oh, Mounce includes derivatives as footnotes to his vocab lists, so that's a shortcut,
but a good dictionary is all you really need.

Greek Geek Zondervan has a workbook called *A Summer
Greek Reader*, which has some charts with
excellent mnemonic devices for all words that
occur from fifty to twenty times.

Bernie Con, I also like to learn cognates together. (Or
perhaps more accurately, wish I had done as I
discover them down-the-track!) It feels like I'm
reinforcing the one idea from a couple of angles
at once.

Con Campbell Yes, cognate-learning is an approach that
works for many people.

Joshua Kuswadi Hi Con. One thing I found helpful was learning vocabulary from lists. Sometimes know-
ing where a word was on a page helped me
remember it. Or that, for example, μέρος came
after μέλος.

Con Campbell Hi Joshua, I found the same thing. Lists seem
especially good for visual learners.

Gazman   Con — reviewing out loud, off lists, with a big whiteboard, with hooks, actions etc. etc. etc., WITH A FRIEND regularly is the only way for me (maybe it has more to do with being an extrovert, not a bookish introvert as a certain bishop described a lot of his Sydney clergy, or perhaps it has more to do with my own lack of discipline or my ADHD???).

One more idea: possibly should have been most obvious to me — the way for me that I retain stuff, especially Greek, is BY TEACHING it. My number one suggestion is to either tutor someone, or start a small group, or get a job at a worthy institution (soft option really).

Con Campbell   Good point, Gary. Teaching helps.

Chapter 5

Practice Your Parsing

Practice makes perfect. Or aorist.
Or present. Or ... what *is* that verb?

It is a simple thing, yet makes a profound difference. Modern English fails to differentiate between "you" singular and "you" plural. So, growing up in an individualistic culture, every time I read "you" in my Bible, I thought it applied to me individually. Greek helped me to appreciate how many "yous" applied to believers collectively. So I began to develop an appreciation of the importance of the church and of the shared responsibilities and privileges we had that had been lacking until then.

Colossians 3:15 is typical of a verse we read individualistically when, in reality, it is as about our relations with one another. The concluding part of the sentence makes the meaning clear: εἰς ἣν καὶ ἐκλήθητε is unmistakably a second person plural and is underlined by "in one body." The calling to peace is not an individual reference but something we collectively are called to as members of one body. We together have been called to live in peace with one another.

Derek Tidball

If vocabulary is the main stumbling block for keeping your Greek, verb forms are probably close behind. As I mentioned in the previous chapter, it's hard to read Greek if you don't know the vocab (even if everything else is there). So, too, it's hard to read Greek if you can't figure out whether you're looking at an aorist or a present, a subjunctive or an imperative. Obviously the difference between these things matters; not only will your reading of a passage suffer if you think an aorist is a present, or a subjunctive is an imperative, but your exegesis and teaching will undoubtedly be affected as well. And it would be a clanger to mistake a noun for a verb, though most of us have done that once or twice!

But how realistic is this? All those paradigms! How will you stay on top? I don't expect pastors to be writing out Greek verb tables every week for the next thirty years. Well, two things come to mind here. First, it *is* possible to improve and maintain your knowledge of verb forms over the long haul. Second, it is even possible to *master* the verb table. Imagine that! Knowing *all* the verb forms and being able to parse any verb that comes your way.

Yes, it is possible. The Greek verb table is big, but it's not infinite. While vocabulary does seem impossible to master, with over five thousand different words in the New Testament and two thousand of those only appearing once, the verb table is not nearly as intimidating. Sure, it may look difficult, but it does have an end. It can be mastered, if you want to take it that far. But even if you don't do that, most people can achieve a good knowledge of the paradigms.

Once you've learned the language and are just trying to maintain your skills in the midst of a busy life and ministry, it will help to develop a simple method for keeping your paradigms sharp that is easy and takes little time.

Here's one such method. When you do your ten to thirty minutes of Greek reading each day, practice your parsing. One way to do this is to read through a verse or a few verses, then go back through the text and parse each verb therein. This may take a little time if your verb paradigms are rusty, but once you get them into shape, it doesn't take long. All you need to say to yourself is, for example, "Present active indicative, third person plural, λέγω." Do this for each verb (including participles and infinitives). Even if you know straight away what you're looking at, by deliberately going through and parsing each form, you will keep your recall sharp.

You don't want to end up *sort of* recognizing verb forms, but not being able to spell out what they are — that's a sign of un-keeping your Greek! Once you've parsed each verb form in the verse or verses you're looking at, it's good to check your accuracy with the use of your software program (if you use one). Or you might check your parsing of each verb as you go through them. Here's how I do this exercise: I will read a slab of Greek in Accordance (a paragraph or so), then go back and quickly parse each verb form in my head. Right after I parse each verb, I move the cursor over the verb to check that my parsing was correct.

Here's another tip for those who are serious about improving their verb paradigms and want to increase their ability with verbs quickly. First, perform the exercise above, parsing each verb form that you find in your daily Greek reading. As you check your verb parsing, however, take note of any forms that you parsed incorrectly. When you've finished your Greek reading, try to master the paradigms that went wrong. For example, if you have incorrectly parsed an aorist passive subjunctive, sit down with a piece of paper and a pen and write out the aorist passive subjunctive paradigm several times (using λύω for the stem). Write out the paradigm until you feel you know it backwards. This may take some time, but as I said, doing this is for those who are serious about getting their verbs into shape. If you follow this workout diligently, your verb-paradigm weaknesses will eventually disappear.

The two tips above are designed to hook your verb-paradigm learning into the regular Greek reading that you do. That way, your verb practice will feel relevant, but also containable. Rather than trying to master the whole verb table in an undifferentiated way, you work on parts of it, as guided by the verbal occurrences in the texts you read. Divide and conquer!

I have one other tip. This is not something I have done, but a retired minister who kept his Greek right to the end of his formal ministry shared it with me. Every year, he set aside one whole day and relearned his entire verb paradigms. He wrote them out, practiced the rusty ones, and reinforced the ones he remembered. For a whole day. Might be worth a try if you need a quick whipping into shape.

Summary: While the Greek verb table can seem intimidating, with one or two simple practices it can be mastered. This will lead to a greatly enhanced ability to read Greek.

Blog Responses

Jason You know, I was tracking right along with you for the first four posts of this series because I was doing all these things. Now you're challenging me to do something hard! But I also know that this is something I have neglected and need to do. Thanks for the kick I needed.

Mike Aubrey My agreement with this one really depends on what a person's goals are. In terms of keeping your Greek and not losing it, it's a good idea; but if we're talking about keeping your Greek in terms of truly internalizing the language like any other language, paradigms are less helpful. But I know that most people don't have the goal of internalizing Hellenistic Greek the same way one would a modern second language.

Con Campbell Fair point, Mike. I think you're right that most people will not be aiming to internalize Greek, though it's a great aim to aspire to. I think my approach is not necessarily opposed to internalization, because the best way to achieve that is to read the text. A lot. That's why I suggest reading first, but then going back over the verbs. Kind of a hybrid approach — best of both worlds perhaps?

Mark Stevens Thanks Con. I spoke with a friend who has taught Greek for some time and he suggested that a paradigm a week might be better than one day a year — especially for internalising. By the way, I am still a bit miffed about the software! How realistic is it that a minister will become proficient in Greek when there are so many demands in parish ministry? I wonder if this is where software helps.

Con Campbell Hi Mark, thanks for your comments and questions. Regarding software, remember that I said this only applies to your dedicated Greek reading of ten minutes a day. I wasn't saying you shouldn't use it "in full" for other things. Cheers.

Alan Kurschner Dr. Campbell, these are great language tips. I took an independent course just on verbal aspect at Gordon Conwell and your book *Verbal Aspect, the Indicative Mood, and Narrative* was required reading. It was a helpful primer for Porter's tome.

I alternate my Greek and Hebrew/Aramaic every day. One task I have been doing now for about two years is once a week I do an exhaustive analysis of a single Greek and Hebrew

verse in this order: morphological, lexical, diagramming, grammatical, and discourse analysis
(with emphasis on the grammatical level to
keep those syntactical categories fresh).

I find this helps me to keep a balance
between translating and grammatical analysis.
This may sound like a lot of work but I find that
it takes me a half hour or more to go through all
of these levels of analysis.

Con Campbell Thanks for sharing that, Alan. It sounds like a
great workout!

Chapter 6

READ FAST

It's the vibe of the thing.

It is important for students and preachers of God's Word to work with Greek concordances to carefully pursue the meaning of words in their context. Reading only English translations can make us captive to misinformation. For example, sometimes a translation will transliterate a word instead of translating it. Μυστήριον is one such word. It usually appears in English translations as "mystery." But is that what it really means, or is that just turning the Greek letters into English letters? A "mystery" in English is something puzzling or strange, even mysteriously unknowable. But within New Testament times the word meant "a secret" – something hidden that has now been made known by revelation. The great "secret" that God revealed through Paul was that Christ was among the Gentiles.

Phillip D. Jensen

This advice needs to be tempered by the next chapter, but it is pretty straightforward: read Greek *quickly*. At least some of the time. The idea is that it can be frustrating and demoralizing to be always reading Greek slowly, paying attention to every detail. Reading slowly is important (see the next chapter), but so is reading quickly. I benefit from mixing it up.

Skim Reading

Lots of people know how to skim read (in English). The idea is that you can pick out the main points of the book or article that you're reading without taking in every detail. This is by no means *careful* reading—the type required for research, for example—but can be an easy way to get a handle on, or a summary of, what the author is saying. Reading everything carefully can sometimes be demoralizing, depending on your level of interest in the topic. Sometimes we just want a grasp of what the article is about, or what an author's conclusions are, or what the basic plot of a novel is. A careful reading might require more time and effort than we can really afford for certain books or articles. We'd prefer to spend our "careful reading time" on other things. So, you see, there is a place for skim reading, though sometimes we need to work out what reading materials deserve a "skim read" and which ones deserve careful reading.

But how is it done? For some people, it just starts to happen naturally. The more you read, the more you get a feel for how to discern the big ideas and to identify the material that's supportive rather than crucial. Every author has crucial points to make and uses supportive material to serve those points. As you get a feel for that, you might become confident enough to skip over the supportive material and focus on the crucial ideas.

If I'm skim reading a theological book (ooh, that sounds wrong, doesn't it?). Ok, if I'm skim reading a book about helicopters, I'll normally read the introduction and then the conclusion, to get a synopsis of the book. Then I'll get an overview of each chapter the same way. Then I'll skim through each paragraph to find out what each one is about. Good writing normally restricts one main point for each paragraph, so it's just a matter of working out what that main point is. By doing that, you can quickly work out how the argument of the chapter is progressing by stringing together the main points of each paragraph. Once you've done this for each chapter, you've skim read the whole book! You can know what the main points and arguments are without getting caught up in the details.

Greek Skimming

Now, what does all this have to do with Greek? The tip I'm suggesting in this chapter is that it can be helpful to skim read Greek in a similar way to our skim reading in English. Not that we would skim read whole Greek books in the same way that we might do English books. The parallel has to do with *speed* and getting the gist of what you're reading, without slowing down for the details. Again, I'm not suggesting that you read Greek like this all the time! On the contrary, there are occasions for reading Greek very carefully, just as some English books and articles need to be read carefully. But there are also occasions to read quickly; it helps us in English, and it can help us with Greek too.

When we read Greek quickly, it helps us get the "vibe" of the language. To get the vibe of something, you need frequent exposure to it, but also some comprehension of the bigger picture. By reading quickly through larger portions of Greek, it's possible to gain an appreciation for the macro-patterns of the language, the larger syntactical shapes, and the way clauses hang together.

Reading quickly will also help you to "internalize" the language in a way that slow and careful reading may not. To internalize a language means that you no longer treat it as an abstract "code" to be deciphered. Rather, it becomes more like a song you know really well. You just know it; you don't have to think about the lyrics or the melody—it's just there. While many of us may never achieve true internalization of Greek, taking steps toward it is still a useful thing. By quickly reading larger slabs of Greek, parts of the language are internalized, because it forces you to hold in your head connections between clauses and the various bits and pieces that are needed for the wider unit to make sense. In other words, reading quickly helps you to think about Greek as a tool for the communication of connected ideas, not just isolated words — one next to the other.

Reading quickly also feels more like you're actually *reading* because you're taking in more content and therefore piecing together the ideas and the wider message of the text. This is how we read in English: we read for meaning and the interconnection of ideas. We don't pause for a painstaking analysis of every word (unless you're a lawyer!). When it feels like we're actually *reading*, Greek will be more enjoyable and less like tooth extraction.

At this point you might be thinking: "That's all well and good. I'd love to read Greek more quickly, but I don't know enough Greek to do that!" Admittedly, everyone is different, but you might be surprised at how much you can piece together just from reading larger slabs in context. You can work out a lot of what's going on just from the context. As they say, context covers over a multitude of evils!

When you try this, just sit down with a Greek New Testament (perhaps open it to a section of one of the Gospels) for ten minutes or so and have a stab at reading. Aim for a good ten lines or so — no more than one minute for each line of Greek. You might want to prepare with some vocabulary beforehand, using Burer & Miller's *A New Reader's Lexicon of the Greek New Testament* or something equivalent. But even if you don't, just skip over words you don't recognize and go for the vibe. You don't need to know every word to do this exercise — you're skimming, after all. If there are words you don't know, move on to parts that you *can* translate and go for the gist of the passage. Remember, the goal here is not to nail everything in the passage, but to read *quickly*. The more you practice this, the easier it will get, and the more familiar the language will feel overall. I always enjoy reading Greek this way; try it for yourself!

In fact, why not try it out right now? There's a short text below to skim read. I suggest trying to read the whole passage in no more than five minutes. Read it out loud, and take in as much

meaning as you can in five minutes. Don't worry about words you
don't know; just aim for speed. Focus on the bold words, which
will outline the gist of the passage.

Ὁ δὲ Ἰησοῦς ἀπεκρίνατο αὐτοῖς· ὁ **πατήρ** μου ἕως ἄρτι
ἐργάζεται κἀγὼ ἐργάζομαι· διὰ τοῦτο οὖν μᾶλλον **ἐζήτουν αὐτὸν**
οἱ **Ἰουδαῖοι ἀποκτεῖναι**, ὅτι οὐ μόνον ἔλυεν τὸ σάββατον, ἀλλὰ
καὶ **πατέρα ἴδιον ἔλεγεν** τὸν **θεὸν** ἴσον ἑαυτὸν ποιῶν τῷ θεῷ.
Ἀπεκρίνατο οὖν ὁ Ἰησοῦς καὶ ἔλεγεν αὐτοῖς· ἀμὴν ἀμὴν λέγω
ὑμῖν, οὐ δύναται ὁ **υἱὸς ποιεῖν ἀφ' ἑαυτοῦ** οὐδὲν ἐὰν μή τι βλέπῃ
τὸν πατέρα ποιοῦντα· ἃ γὰρ ἂν ἐκεῖνος ποιῇ, ταῦτα καὶ ὁ υἱὸς
ὁμοίως ποιεῖ. ὁ γὰρ **πατὴρ φιλεῖ** τὸν **υἱὸν καὶ πάντα δείκνυσιν**
αὐτῷ ἃ αὐτὸς ποιεῖ, καὶ μείζονα τούτων δείξει αὐτῷ ἔργα, ἵνα
ὑμεῖς θαυμάζητε. **ὥσπερ** γὰρ ὁ **πατὴρ ἐγείρει** τοὺς **νεκροὺς** καὶ
ζῳοποιεῖ, οὕτως καὶ ὁ **υἱὸς** οὓς θέλει **ζῳοποιεῖ**. (John 5:17–21)

Summary: Read Greek quickly and dig the vibe, man.

Blog Responses

Mike Aubrey Ooh, I really like this one. I have my own varia-
tion. I listen to the recordings from http://www
.greeklatinaudio.com/ and follow along with my
GNT.

Con Campbell Thanks Mike, that's a great idea.

Laura I like this one too ... WAY more than the last
one! It's fun to read Greek as though I'm great
at it, instead of slogging through it with the reality of my pitiful two semesters plus one summer
term of Greek hanging over my head. Fake it 'til
you make it, huh?

What a blessing and encouragement this
series is! Thanks for putting all this work in.

Alan Kurschner Mixing it up helps tremendously! Thanks.

Lionel Windsor Hi Con. Something I've discovered (far too late) is that the benefits of reading quickly can be multiplied tenfold if you read out loud. Reading aloud helps you to feel the language — its shape, its tones, its accents, etc. I regularly read a chapter out loud as quickly as possible, without stopping to look up vocab. My main goal is to maintain accuracy in my pronunciation and accents while getting faster and faster. This really helps the language to soak in.

Con Campbell Good one, Lionel.

Jason Chamberlain I make a point of reading more from my Reader's Greek New Testament daily. For a while I was just reading a paragraph or two every day, which was good. However, I think I was agonizing over some parts too much.

This year I am reading a chapter a day. I've made the Greek NT my primary devotional reading. I have found that this has helped me read faster and with greater comprehension (getting the vibe, if you will). I also find that this has helped me rely less on the footnotes as the vocabulary sinks in better with more exposure in a shorter time.

Overall, I feel like I am "really reading" much more than I was before. Now that I've seen how this process has worked in Greek, I am inspired to put forth the same effort for Hebrew. There is simply no substitute for time in the text.

Con Campbell Great to hear that, Jason.

Scott D. Andersen Thanks for the further advice. I really look forward to this book and enjoy access to the posts you've made so far.

Marsha Cleaveland I began sight-reading Greek in my first semester of study. Because I have lived abroad for years, learning languages "in situ," I understand the benefit of massive exposure to a language, in spite of a lack of precision in understanding. This gave me three immediate benefits: 1) I frequently saw the vocabulary I was working so hard to learn — in context; 2) I grew to have an organic feel for the syntactical structure before being harassed with all the syntactic tags; 3) I learned to quickly spot the vocabulary "stems" and approximate a meaning in spite of not knowing how to parse every suffix.

I began with the gospel of John, and within eight months had read all four Gospels. This approach has the added value of seeing similar vocabulary repeated through the Gospels, as well as rereading familiar stories, usually without extremely long, convoluted sentences.

A chapter a day of sight-reading is my current goal, in addition to the advanced Greek workbooks and grammars I am using. I find that reading it last thing at night cements my learning and allows my mind to contemplate the Greek from a relaxed state.

Chapter 7

READ SLOW

Slow and steady wins the race.

What was the most useful thing I did in theological college? Learn Greek, without question! Through reading the original texts I have learned things and noticed points and asked questions I would never have seen otherwise; it's like watching colour TV after years of watching black-and-white.

One important example for me has been questions whose form suggests their answer (technically questions beginning with μή or οὐ). To notice that the questions in 1 Corinthians 12:29 – 30 all imply the answer no clarifies that every believer should not expect to have all the Spirit's gifts, and that not every believer should expect to have any individual gift — thus freeing believers to be the people God has equipped them to be. Similarly, the force of Matthew 18:33, a question implying the answer yes is strongly suggestive that one who has been forgiven a great debt should be ready to forgive anyone in debt to them — and this strengthens the point of the parable of the unforgiving servant.

Steve Walton

While it's a good thing to practice reading Greek quickly (see the last chapter), it's important to balance that with reading slowly. Not because reading slowly is necessarily an inherently good thing, but the point is that you practice reading Greek *carefully*.

Like any skill, there's a wide gap between "rough-n-ready," "close-enough-is-good-enough" ability and precise, accurate execution. For serious musicians, the gap between those two standards makes all the difference. For some other professions, that gap is the difference between proficiency and failure—such as in architecture or engineering. For yet other professions, that gap can mean the difference between life and death—such as for doctors or chemists. Without wanting to exaggerate the point—knowing Greek is not normally a matter of life or death!—the difference between someone who really is on top of Greek and someone who is at risk of losing it comes down to the details.

Yes, the "vibe" of the language is important (see the last chapter); having an intuitive sense of how Greek hangs together is great. But these things are not meant to substitute for a genuine grasp of the details of the language. The best Greek students are the ones who get the "vibe" of the language and *also* have a strong grip on the vocabulary, grammar, and syntax. The key way to reinforce and sharpen your grasp of the "details" of Greek is to practice reading slowly. This can easily be incorporated into our daily Greek reading, as can reading quickly. The key is to mix it up so that your daily Greek reading is fast on occasion, and slow at other times.

The irony is that reading slowly and carefully will ultimately enable you to read quickly and easily. That's because true reading ability in Greek is only possible when you are familiar and comfortable with the details. I remember clearly when I learned this about music. At the time I was practicing saxophone hard and was trying to get to the next level with my technique. I recall reading an interview with one of my favourite musicians, Branford Marsalis, in *Downbeat Magazine*. Part of the interview dealt with his practice regimen, and I was struck by one thing he said. He insisted that the best way to gain great technique—and to be able to play fast with control — was to practice scales *really* slowly. I mean ridiculously slowly. The idea was to use a metronome (to keep time), set on forty beats per minute, and to make sure that every single note was played exactly on the beat.

When I tried this, I realized that I could play quickly, but not necessarily accurately. The notes did not fall exactly where they should have. And so, from that point on I practiced scales really slowly, aiming for accuracy. After only a few weeks of this practice, I felt my technique and control dramatically improve. I still credit that exercise as the foundation of my saxophone technique. The same thing applies to Greek. Reading slowly and carefully will give you precision and accuracy, which will result in better all-round performance in the long run.

When you read Greek slowly, make sure it really is *slow*. Take care with the details, so that you know what every word contributes to each clause. Parse every verb and consider its significance. Examine each clause, paying attention to where each clause begins and ends. Work out if the clause is independent or subordinate. Take notice of conjunctions. Look for the subtleties that often go unnoticed. By really slowing down and examining everything you see with care and patience, before long you'll find that your ability with the details of the language will vastly improve. More than that, you'll notice what the text is *really* saying, not just what you think it ought to be saying.

Reading slowly with care can be rewarding, since it is through this kind of reading that we can find in the Greek text the sorts of things that many of us learned Greek for in the first place: little hidden nuances and exegetical insights that are conveyed by the Greek, but are so often lost in English translation; the richer, deeper comprehension of the text; and appreciation of the structure of sentences. Such insights don't normally occur without slow and careful reading.

Summary: Read Greek slowly, and watch your skill increase.

Blog Responses

Joseph Griffin Con, I really appreciate your series of posts related to keeping your Greek. The tips that I have already put into use have been very helpful so far. I really appreciate your service to me and others through these posts.

Con Campbell Thanks Joseph, I'm glad it's been useful.

Jason Chamberlain Thank you for the tip. Now I need to make time to do this. I have kidded myself by thinking that a lot of reading every day is enough. However, I find myself unsure enough on the forms that I realize that I need to find a way to make this happen.

Chapter 8

USE YOUR SENSES

Greek is a language, not just words on a page.

> I tell my students to use all the senses they can to learn Greek. If they could put olive oil and a dash of grilled pork on their papers, that would help too (just kidding on that one). Writing out the Greek and saying it aloud is very important for this task of retaining the language.
>
> *Daniel B. Wallace*

Increasingly, teachers are harnessing different methods for learning Greek, including catering to different learning styles and utilizing the power of our senses for language acquisition. Recent studies have revealed that the most potent sense for the stimulation of memory is our sense of smell. Unfortunately, it is a little difficult to incorporate smell into our learning of Greek, though you might be able to think of some ways. Personally, some of my fondest Greek memories are associated with Kalamata olives and feta cheese, but that doesn't really help with paradigms.

Speaking and Hearing

The sense that could be exploited more is that of hearing. Because Greek is normally treated as a dead language (though it is far from it!), there is often little interest shown in pronouncing it or hearing it read aloud. This is a great shame. Speaking Greek out loud can be a useful way to internalize the language. Hearing Greek spoken aloud causes us to process the information in a different way to reading, and therefore strengthens our overall comprehension. This will be the case for most people, but especially for aural learners.

As we read our Greek New Testament each day, it is a good idea to spend at least some of that time reading aloud. Personally, I think it is also worth making sure that we stress each word according to the placement of its accent. Accents are often ignored by students, as we're told that they're not important for the meaning of the text. But in pronunciation we need to stress *one* of the syllables of each word, so why not stress the syllable that is supposed to be stressed? It doesn't take too much effort when reading an accented text (it's much easier than working out for ourselves where the accents are supposed to go), and it will sound much more like real Greek. After all, Greek *is* a real language that is supposed to sound a certain way. In addition, that kind of attention to the details of the text will ultimately aid our absorption of the language.

One of my blog readers, Mike Aubrey, suggests listening to Greek being read from www.greeklatinaudio.com while following along in the Greek New Testament. This is a great way to incorporate multiple senses in reading Greek and has the added benefit of forcing you to read at pace. You could listen and read silently, or listen and pronounce the Greek at the same time.

Reading Greek text is not the only thing that can be done aloud. It is also worth practicing paradigms and vocabulary aloud. I know some people who can rattle off whole verb tables in a few seconds, and that is their way of keeping the information in their heads. The beauty of this, of course, is that paradigms can be practiced anytime, anywhere (with the exception perhaps of the dentist chair). There is also a rhythm to many of the Greek paradigms, and rhythm is always good! If you got rhythm, who could ask for anything more?

Singing?

It seems that singing Greek is all the rage at the moment. While some musicians are capable of scat-singing with biblical text, that's not what I mean. Kenneth Berding has developed a resource called *Sing and Learn New Testament Greek*, which provides a way to learn and remember Greek grammar forms through simple songs. The project includes songs for indicative verb endings, participles, infinitives, imperatives, contract forms, and prepositions. Apparently, the songs are so simple that students who have used them complain about waking up in the middle of the night with the songs running through their heads! Now, that's what I call one of those *good* problems!

Writing

One of my favourite techniques for learning and reviewing paradigms is to write them out by hand. I find that having to reproduce the paradigms is much more effective than just reviewing them. Reviewing paradigms really only reminds us of the forms, but it does not force us to learn them. To reproduce them, however, we must *know* the forms. I like to write out a verb paradigm and only refer to the "answer" once the whole paradigm is complete. If there are mistakes, I'll review the paradigm, then write it out a few more times. I'm a visual learner, so writing and then reviewing works well for me and is good for recognizing the many patterns that exist throughout the Greek verb table.

Summary: Your senses are powerful tools for learning and retaining Greek.

Blog Responses

Redpooba I could not agree more about the speaking and hearing of the language. That is why I went to Greece — to fully immerse myself with the language and bathe in it. But I disagree with your line about Greek food: fresh olives could help you learn Greek. Greek babies learn Greek while eating olives; why can't we? Perhaps olives, feta, and "Greek coffee" could be utilized in the classroom to assist in the learning. If not, at least the class would be full because of the tasty treats.

Con Campbell Ok, you got me there, Redpooba. More olives and feta!

Don Berman Thanks Con. I believe that sounding out the Greek certainly helps me. I am attempting to retain my first-year Greek. I am using my Greek Bible alongside a parallel Bible (with English), but I suspect this in the long run is not going to solidify my Greek as an independent skill. God bless.

Marsha Cleaveland My first Greek prof took the class to a local Greek Orthodox festival to get a broader feel for the language and culture as it is today. Also, I enjoyed expanding my immersion in the language through watching a series from the public library on the ruins of ancient Greece. Anything to stimulate the "Greek" side of the brain — feta cheese and olives included!

Chapter 9

GET YOUR GREEK BACK

If you did it once, you can do it again. And it will be easier this time.

In some preaching circles I frequently hear well-intended warnings against using Greek in sermons. "Don't ever quote the original," some say, "or you might distance your people from the Word of God or bring glory to yourself instead of the Lord." I disagree and wonder how much of this criticism derives from critics' own personal awkwardness with Koine Greek. Of course, it's possible to overdo any good thing, but as I've thought about it over the years—having once staunchly upheld this view myself—I've now come to the following opinion. All of our people know that the New Testament was written in Greek, not English. They are hardly going to be surprised that the preacher can read it in the original. In fact, I am sure they would be quite disappointed if they realised that he or she could not. There is every chance, then, that using Greek not only in sermon preparation but also in delivery will actually attune your people to the language and help them over time feel less, not more, distant from the original text. The more they hear it in passing—not just in isolated words but in whole clauses—the more they will know that Greek is a rather simple language we know an awful lot about and, just as important, they will see that the original has, for the most part, been very well rendered in the English text in front of them.

Not using the Greek in public has the potential to create a mysterious distance between the pew Bible and an unknown original. As an analogy, imagine the weekly gatherings of the American Victor Hugo Appreciation Society (I assume one exists). I cannot imagine the president of the society not knowing French and occasionally quoting whole sentences in the original as the group discusses the beautiful way, for instance, Hugo describes Bishop Myriel's treatment of Jean Valjean at the beginning of *Les Misérables*. The sounds and nuances of the French original will bring an immediacy and intimacy to the text even if most of the group can only follow it in English. Well done—and, of course, this requires that the preacher is comfortable with the Greek New Testament—the same will be true of our own occasional use of the original language in sermons.

John P. Dickson

Backsliding

It can be demoralizing to feel as if you're backsliding, no matter what the skill is. You've put in the work, and you've reached a certain level of proficiency; you know what it feels like to be able to do certain things that you once couldn't do—and it feels good! But then a while later, for whatever reason, you realize you're no longer at that level of ability; you can no longer do some of the things you once did. That doesn't feel so good. In fact, it can be downright depressing.

There's a chance I've talked about music too often in this book, but bear with one last indulgence. I know firsthand what it feels like to go backward as a saxophonist. It really sucks. And I know other musicians who've had the same experience, and they hate it as much as I do. No one likes going backward. I think it has to do with the fact that it took so much work to get where you once were, but it can be lost so easily. When we work hard for something, we want to be moving forward, not just retracing our steps and catching up to where we've already been before. And then there's the hard reality that your performance is affected; you're more limited than you once were.

If you've experienced backsliding in your Greek ability, you know what I'm talking about. It's demoralizing, isn't it? In fact, it can be debilitating. Some people will be so discouraged by their backsliding that they will just give it all up. Keeping your Greek can be so hard, and the journey fraught with disappointments like backsliding, that life will be easier without it. If that's what you're thinking ... *wait!* Don't give up yet. You can get your Greek back. Yes, it will take some work. Yes, it will be hard at times. But it will be worth it. When you're on top of it again, reading the Greek New Testament will be its own reward. You'll have access to the nuances of the text that were previously hidden. You'll make informed exegetical decisions based on Greek syntax. It will be worth it!

While backsliding hurts, there is a plus side to knowing what it feels like. It makes me determined not to let it happen! As much as possible, I make sure I'm playing music regularly, because I know that if I don't, I won't like the consequences. If you know what it feels like to slide back in your Greek, you can use that to your advantage. You want to avoid that pain. If you're at risk of it happening again, think about the consequences. Don't let yourself go backward again. Gather your energy and focus; become determined to maintain your ability.

Reversing the Backslide

You need to make a decision at this point, if you haven't already. I hope you're ready to reverse the backslide. Assuming that you are ready to do this, let's explore some ways to reverse the downward spiral.

I suppose there are many things you could do to get your Greek on the onward and upward again. Here are a few suggestions.

1. Take heart! It will come to you more quickly than it did the first time. It's easier to remember the Greek you've forgotten than it was to learn it in the first place. This is true for most learned skills; once you get back into the swing of things, your memory starts to access that old information more and more quickly. The knowledge you once had is sitting in the back of your brain like old books gathering dust in the back of a library. They're back there somewhere, though they're hard to find. But once those books get back into regular circulation, the dust disappears and they are easy to find. It's just a question of getting stuck into that library and finding what you're looking for. Get that library card out and put it to good use!

Even if you have let your Greek go completely cold, once you start working it up again, you should find it will get progressively easier. Don't be discouraged by relearning what you've forgotten. Instead, be encouraged that you'll learn Greek faster than those who are learning it from scratch!

2. It's a bit like muscle-training. It hurts at first and can be quite a shock to the system. There may not be any visible results right away. But with perseverance, you will make progress, one step at a time. With perseverance and regular "working out," your Greek will gradually get into shape. And like muscle-training, you're better off taking small steps to start with, lest you hurt yourself! But as you get stronger, turn up the volume (to mix metaphors) and work with more resistance. Greater resistance is essential for your muscles to develop further, and your Greek will get stronger by reading progressively harder Greek. It won't improve much by only doing the easy stuff that you already know; those muscles need to be strained in order to enhance their development.

3. Keep it real. While a positive attitude will serve you better than being overly negative, still you need to be realistic about your strengths and weaknesses. If you have gaps, recognize them and address them. If you make parsing mistakes, practice your paradigms. If you've forgotten lots of vocabulary, give that some extra attention. There's no point pretending you're in better shape than you really are. Do the work: read Greek every day, review your vocabulary and paradigms, and read every day ... Put into practice the tips I've already suggested in the previous chapters of this book.

Remember: the main difference between someone who keeps their Greek and someone who loses it is the commitment to give it a little time each day. Are you up for it?

Summary: Reverse the decline, and your Greek will shine. ☺

Blog Responses

Mark Stevens Con, I find it relatively easy to remember the paradigms. However, what are your tips for remembering what the paradigms refer to and how they are used? For instance, how do I remember what an aorist or participle means to the actual sentence structure? I often find my translation is on the right track but I have missed a tense or mood somewhere along the line!

Thanks for these posts; they have been helpful and challenging!

Con Campbell Mark, it sounds like you would appreciate some help with syntax. Wallace is a good resource for helping to think through the different uses of particular parts of speech. Check it out.

Sandy Grant The thing that has helped me most recently is buying *A Reader's Greek New Testament* — one of those NTs that instead of giving you the textual apparatus, footnotes every piece of NT vocab that occurs less than thirty times in the text. The time saved in looking up lexicons is enormous and has made me more inclined to pull out the Greek and to practise!

Con Campbell Thanks, Sandy. Yes, some have said they appreciate that tool, and it appears to be of genuine value.

Chris Lindsay Con, great series. Thanks. I really appreciate how you've broken down "keeping your Greek" into manageable micro-steps.

Chapter 10

PUTTING IT ALL TOGETHER

Make it a part of life.

Preachers are always looking for simple and preachable texts. But the syntax of our sermon must stem from the Greek syntax of the text, not the English syntax. Titus 2:12 speaks of the grace of God teaching "us to renounce ungodliness and worldly passions, and to live self-controlled, upright, and godly lives in the present age" (ESV). It is wonderfully balanced and preachable: the negative "to renounce ungodliness and worldly passions" is balanced by the positive "to live self-controlled, upright, and godly lives." The trouble is that the Greek is different: "to renounce" is an aorist participle and "to live" is a subjunctive. Thus, Robert H. and William D. Mounce translate it similar to the KJV: "having denied the ungodliness and the worldly passions, we should live in a self-controlled manner, and justly and reverently." The Greek takes seriously our renunciation in conversion as the basis for the new life that we are consequentially being taught to pursue. It may not be as balanced as it appears in some translations, but it is theologically and pastorally more profound.

Phillip D. Jensen

I decided it might be useful to describe how keeping my Greek works out in my life. At first I wasn't going to write this chapter because of two concerns. First, I don't want you to think that there's only one way of putting it all together. Just because my pattern of doing things works for me doesn't mean it's going to work for you, and I'd rather you work it out for yourself.

Second, I'm worried that this might come across as boastful. I have a healthy pattern that keeps my Greek in pretty good shape, but I don't want you to think that I'm bignoting myself for saying this. In the end, I've included this chapter because I hope it might be useful. Seeing how it all fits together in at least one person's real life could be a good thing. It might also be helpful to show how to keep one's Greek alongside other languages. So, here goes.

My Pattern

I use the term *pattern* because it's less boring than *routine* and more flexible than *regimen*. This is what I normally do, five or six days a week. I rise early and spend the first hour of the day in Bible reading and prayer, and I use my Bible reading time to practice my languages. Not everyone likes to combine their devotional time with language practice, but it works for me.

As is the case with many people who read the New Testament in Greek, I have more than one language to maintain. Many pastors and students will also be keen to read some Hebrew, and theologians may also need to practice their German and other languages. I try to read a little of each of my languages each day. I have an Old Testament reading and a New Testament reading going simultaneously, and I alternate each day between them. At the moment, I'm finishing off 1 Kings and Acts. I read from these texts using Accordance, and I have a tab open for each language I want to read, with each tab set at 1 Kings in my OT window, and each tab set at Acts in my NT window. A screenshot of each can be seen below. The advantage of using tabs is that I see only one language at a time, which prevents cheating. I only use my cursor to check vocabulary when I absolutely have to.

My pattern at the moment is to read a few verses from 1 Kings in Hebrew, then check an English translation. Then I'll read the next verses in Aramaic, then the next few in Greek, the next few in German, and the next few in French. When I'm reading the New Testament the next day, I'll start with Greek, then read the next few verses from a Hebrew NT, Syriac, German, and French. The advantages of this pattern are that I can take in a fair slab of the Bible, which is good for devotional purposes, and each language is read each day. A disadvantage is that it means I won't read the whole of Acts in Greek, since I've read some of it in the other languages instead. But I'm OK with that tradeoff.

As I follow this pattern, I'll tend to focus more on one language than the others, but I switch the focus language around from day to day so that each language gets a more focused treatment at least once a week. But even so, every language is still read each day. I'll also incorporate the methods and practices that I have advocated in this book as part of my pattern. For example, I'll alternate between reading large slabs of text quickly and smaller sections slowly.

This pattern has served me well for several years, and I look forward to reading the Bible this way each day. It keeps my Greek (and other languages) ticking over, and is not too difficult to sustain. But it's not for everyone. Figure out what is going to work best for you. I only offer my own pattern as an example to give you some ideas and a picture of what it can look like when everything is put together. Remember, you only need ten minutes of quality reading time each day to keep your Greek.

AC 23

Verse 1 of 35

23:1 Ἀτενίσας δὲ ὁ Παῦλος τῷ συνεδρίῳ εἶπεν· ἄνδρες ἀδελφοί, ἐγὼ πάσῃ συνειδήσει ἀγαθῇ πεπολίτευμαι τῷ θεῷ ἄχρι ταύτης τῆς ἡμέρας. **2** ὁ δὲ ἀρχιερεὺς Ἁνανίας ἐπέταξεν τοῖς παρεστῶσιν αὐτῷ τύπτειν αὐτοῦ τὸ στόμα. **3** τότε ὁ Παῦλος πρὸς αὐτὸν εἶπεν· τύπτειν σε μέλλει ὁ θεός, τοῖχε κεκονιαμένε· καὶ σὺ κάθῃ κρίνων με κατὰ τὸν νόμον καὶ παρανομῶν κελεύεις με τύπτεσθαι; **4** οἱ δὲ παρεστῶτες εἶπαν· τὸν ἀρχιερέα τοῦ θεοῦ λοιδορεῖς; **5** ἔφη τε ὁ Παῦλος· οὐκ ᾔδειν, ἀδελφοί, ὅτι ἐστὶν ἀρχιερεύς· γέγραπται γὰρ ὅτι ἄρχοντα τοῦ λαοῦ σου οὐκ ἐρεῖς κακῶς. **6** Γνοὺς δὲ ὁ Παῦλος ὅτι τὸ ἓν μέρος ἐστὶν Σαδδουκαίων τὸ δὲ ἕτερον Φαρισαίων ἔκραζεν ἐν τῷ συνεδρίῳ· ἄνδρες ἀδελφοί, ἐγὼ Φαρισαῖός εἰμι, υἱὸς Φαρισαίων, περὶ ἐλπίδος καὶ ἀναστάσεως νεκρῶν [ἐγὼ] κρίνομαι. **7** τοῦτο δὲ αὐτοῦ εἰπόντος ἐγένετο στάσις τῶν Φαρισαίων καὶ Σαδδουκαίων καὶ ἐσχίσθη τὸ πλῆθος. **8** Σαδδουκαῖοι μὲν γὰρ λέγουσιν μὴ εἶναι ἀνάστασιν μήτε ἄγγελον μήτε πνεῦμα, Φαρισαῖοι δὲ ὁμολογοῦσιν τὰ ἀμφότερα. **9** ἐγένετο δὲ κραυγὴ μεγάλη, καὶ ἀναστάντες τινὲς τῶν γραμματέων τοῦ μέρους τῶν Φαρισαίων διεμάχοντο λέγοντες· οὐδὲν κακὸν εὑρίσκομεν ἐν τῷ ἀνθρώπῳ τούτῳ· εἰ δὲ πνεῦμα ἐλάλησεν αὐτῷ ἢ ἄγγελος; **10** Πολλῆς δὲ γινομένης στάσεως φοβηθεὶς ὁ χιλίαρχος μὴ διασπασθῇ ὁ Παῦλος ὑπ' αὐτῶν ἐκέλευσεν τὸ στράτευμα καταβὰν ἁρπάσαι αὐτὸν ἐκ μέσου αὐτῶν ἄγειν τε εἰς τὴν παρεμβολήν. **11** Τῇ δὲ ἐπιούσῃ νυκτὶ ἐπιστὰς αὐτῷ ὁ κύριος εἶπεν· θάρσει· ὡς γὰρ διεμαρτύρω τὰ περὶ ἐμοῦ εἰς Ἰερουσαλήμ, οὕτω σε δεῖ καὶ εἰς Ῥώμην μαρτυρῆσαι.

12 Γενομένης δὲ ἡμέρας, ποιήσαντες συστροφὴν οἱ Ἰουδαῖοι ἀνεθεμάτισαν ἑαυτοὺς λέγοντες μήτε φαγεῖν μήτε πιεῖν ἕως οὗ ἀποκτείνωσιν τὸν Παῦλον. **13** ἦσαν δὲ πλείους τεσσεράκοντα οἱ ταύτην τὴν συνωμοσίαν ποιησάμενοι, **14** οἵτινες προσελθόντες τοῖς ἀρχιερεῦσιν καὶ τοῖς πρεσβυτέροις εἶπαν· ἀναθέματι ἀνεθεματίσαμεν ἑαυτοὺς μηδενὸς γεύσασθαι ἕως οὗ ἀποκτείνωμεν τὸν Παῦλον. **15** νῦν οὖν ὑμεῖς ἐμφανίσατε τῷ χιλιάρχῳ σὺν τῷ συνεδρίῳ ὅπως καταγάγῃ αὐτὸν εἰς ὑμᾶς ὡς μέλλοντας διαγινώσκειν ἀκριβέστερον τὰ περὶ αὐτοῦ· ἡμεῖς δὲ πρὸ τοῦ ἐγγίσαι αὐτὸν ἕτοιμοί ἐσμεν τοῦ ἀνελεῖν αὐτόν. **16** Ἀκούσας δὲ ὁ υἱὸς τῆς ἀδελφῆς Παύλου τὴν ἐνέδραν, παραγενόμενος καὶ εἰσελθὼν εἰς τὴν παρεμβολὴν ἀπήγγειλεν τῷ Παύλῳ. **17** προσκαλεσάμενος δὲ ὁ Παῦλος ἕνα τῶν ἑκατονταρχῶν ἔφη· τὸν νεανίαν τοῦτον ἀπάγαγε πρὸς τὸν χιλίαρχον, ἔχει γὰρ ἀπαγγεῖλαί τι αὐτῷ. **18** ὁ μὲν οὖν παραλαβὼν αὐτὸν ἤγαγεν πρὸς τὸν χιλίαρχον καὶ φησίν· ὁ δέσμιος Παῦλος προσκαλεσάμενός με ἠρώτησεν τοῦτον τὸν νεανίσκον ἀγαγεῖν πρὸς σὲ ἔχοντά τι λαλῆσαί σοι. **19** ἐπιλαβόμενος δὲ τῆς χειρὸς αὐτοῦ ὁ χιλίαρχος καὶ ἀναχωρήσας κατ' ἰδίαν ἐπυνθάνετο, τί ἐστιν ὃ ἔχεις ἀπαγγεῖλαί μοι; **20** εἶπεν δὲ ὅτι οἱ Ἰουδαῖοι συνέθεντο τοῦ ἐρωτῆσαί σε ὅπως αὔριον τὸν Παῦλον καταγάγῃς εἰς τὸ συνέδριον ὡς μέλλον τι ἀκριβέστερον πυνθάνεσθαι περὶ αὐτοῦ. **21** σὺ οὖν μὴ πεισθῇς αὐτοῖς· ἐνεδρεύουσιν γὰρ αὐτὸν ἐξ αὐτῶν ἄνδρες πλείους τεσσεράκοντα, οἵτινες ἀνεθεμάτισαν ἑαυτοὺς μήτε φαγεῖν μήτε πιεῖν ἕως οὗ ἀνέλωσιν αὐτόν, καὶ νῦν εἰσιν ἕτοιμοι προσδεχόμενοι τὴν ἀπὸ σοῦ ἐπαγγελίαν. **22** ὁ μὲν οὖν χιλίαρχος ἀπέλυσε τὸν νεανίσκον παραγγείλας μηδενὶ ἐκλαλῆσαι ὅτι ταῦτα ἐνεφάνισας πρός με.

23 Καὶ προσκαλεσάμενός δύο [τινὰς] τῶν ἑκατονταρχῶν εἶπεν· ἑτοιμάσατε στρατιώτας διακοσίους, ὅπως πορευθῶσιν ἕως Καισαρείας, καὶ ἱππεῖς ἑβδομήκοντα καὶ δεξιολάβους διακοσίους ἀπὸ τρίτης ὥρας τῆς νυκτός, **24** κτήνη τε παραστῆσαι ἵνα ἐπιβιβάσαντες τὸν Παῦλον διασώσωσι πρὸς Φήλικα τὸν ἡγεμόνα, **25** γράψας ἐπιστολὴν ἔχουσαν τὸν τύπον τοῦτον· **26** Κλαύδιος Λυσίας τῷ κρατίστῳ ἡγεμόνι Φήλικι χαίρειν. **27** Τὸν ἄνδρα τοῦτον συλλημφθέντα ὑπὸ τῶν Ἰουδαίων καὶ μέλλοντα ἀναιρεῖσθαι ὑπ' αὐτῶν ἐπιστὰς σὺν τῷ στρατεύματι ἐξειλάμην μαθὼν ὅτι Ῥωμαῖός ἐστιν. **28** βουλόμενός τε ἐπιγνῶναι τὴν αἰτίαν δι' ἣν ἐνεκάλουν αὐτῷ, κατήγαγον εἰς τὸ συνέδριον αὐτῶν **29** ὃν εὗρον ἐγκαλούμενον περὶ ζητημάτων τοῦ νόμου αὐτῶν, μηδὲν δὲ ἄξιον θανάτου ἢ δεσμῶν ἔχοντα ἔγκλημα. **30** μηνυθείσης δέ μοι ἐπιβουλῆς εἰς τὸν ἄνδρα ἔσεσθαι ἐξαυτῆς ἔπεμψα πρὸς σὲ παραγγείλας καὶ τοῖς κατηγόροις λέγειν [τὰ] πρὸς αὐτὸν ἐπὶ σοῦ. **31** Οἱ μὲν οὖν στρατιῶται κατὰ τὸ διατεταγμένον αὐτοῖς ἀναλαβόντες τὸν Παῦλον ἤγαγον διὰ νυκτὸς εἰς τὴν Ἀντιπατρίδα, **32** τῇ δὲ ἐπαύριον ἐάσαντες τοὺς ἱππεῖς ἀπέρχεσθαι σὺν αὐτῷ ὑπέστρεψαν εἰς τὴν παρεμβολήν· **33** οἵτινες εἰσελθόντες εἰς τὴν Καισάρειαν καὶ ἀναδόντες τὴν ἐπιστολὴν τῷ ἡγεμόνι παρέστησαν καὶ τὸν Παῦλον αὐτῷ. **34** ἀναγνοὺς

35

HCSB = English; MHNT = Modern Hebrew; PESHNT = Syriac; ELBER = German; NEG79 = French

HCSB = English; TARG-T = Aramaic; LXX1 = Greek; ELBER = German; NEG79 = French

GET IT RIGHT THE FIRST TIME

A stitch in time saves nine.

In my first year of Greek at Biola University, I nearly failed the subject. The professor, Dr. Harry Sturz, had compassion on me and gave me a passing grade. I took a different professor in second-year Greek. He gave us a battery of exams at the beginning of the semester. One exam each week. I failed the first exam. I failed the second exam. I failed the third exam. I failed the fourth exam, but it was a high F! And I got a D on the fifth exam. "Hey", I thought, "I'm really getting this Greek thing down!"

The professor called me into his office and told me that I should check out of Greek. That was the wake-up call I needed. I went down to my dorm room, got on my knees, and confessed to the Lord that I had dragged his name through the mud. I reasoned that since I am in Christ and he is in me, he was failing Greek, too. And even though I was at a Christian school, I was soiling his reputation. I repented of my sin — the sin of mediocrity because I was surrounded by Christians, the sin of thinking that I did not need to do my best since I was a Christian.

I went back to the professor and asked for one more chance. He granted that to me. I ended up getting an A in the class both semesters. It still took me two more years of Greek at Biola before I even felt mildly comfortable with the language, but I had learned my lesson. Now, to be sure, my experience is not everyone's. But, for me, learning Greek became a matter of spiritual discipline. And even though I was very sick in my fourth semester of Greek — so that I missed five and a half weeks of school — I still did well in the course.

I don't consider myself good at languages, but I do consider myself a steward of the life that God has given to me. And I have never recovered from the impact that the Greek New Testament has made on my walk with Christ.

Daniel B. Wallace

When I was a kid, I had no idea what this proverb meant: *A stitch in time saves nine.* What sort of *stitch*? I once had to get some stitches in my leg — is that what it's talking about? And what does *in time* mean? Is it like a drumbeat? And what about *saves nine*? Nine cats? I had no idea. Of course, now that I'm a wise old adult, I understand what the saying means. If your coat starts to develop a tear, one timely stitch will prevent it from tearing further, when the coat will need at least nine stitches to be fixed. One stitch at the right time will save nine stitches later.

The principle can be applied to learning Greek. The more capable you become with Greek when you first learn it, the easier it will be to keep your Greek in the future. I suppose this is really aimed at students who are learning Greek for the first time round, rather than at pastors who need to relearn it. Students should realize that the effort they put in now will have big implications for whether they will struggle to keep their Greek in the future.

The reason for this is simple. Pastors struggle to keep their Greek because they are busy. But the weaker your Greek is to start with, the more time it takes to keep it going. You spend more time looking up vocab and remembering paradigms, not to mention just trying to get the vibe of the thing. It all takes more time than it should. And eventually many pastors will give it up because they can't afford the time anymore. Thus, if your Greek is not strong when you go into ministry, you are far more likely to lose it over time. And the real tragedy is that all those hours you put in while a student will become a waste of time, because you have not retained the language.

If you're a student at seminary, Bible college, or university and are currently studying Greek, you will never have a better time to get it under your belt. I understand that your studies might be busy, and perhaps Greek is not at the top of the pecking order in terms of your priorities. But please take advantage of the fact that you are a student. You get to go to Greek classes, and you are studying it with fellow students. You have exams and assessments to prepare for, and you might have Greek reading classes together. All of these things present a golden opportunity, and once you're no longer a student, it will all vanish. It will be *much* harder to learn more Greek once you're done with your studies, so make it count now.

I know that some theological students struggle with the idea of putting so many hours into acquiring Greek (and Hebrew), while they really want to be learning about the Bible and theology. After all, studying the Bible is about getting to know God better, right? Sometimes all those Greek verb paradigms seem a long way removed from that goal. Keep in mind that you want to know Greek so that you can teach God's Word with depth of understanding, observing its subtleties and nuances, many of which cannot be conveyed in translation.

Greek also enables you to better understand the academic debates about certain verses and passages and to engage with the commentators. They will not have this mysterious secret knowledge over you called Greek, which makes their opinion unquestionable, because you will have access to the same knowledge. You can evaluate the strength of commentators' opinions based on your own understanding of the Greek text. Furthermore, knowing Greek immerses you in the world of the text of the New Testament in a way that is impossible without Greek. All of this is for the purpose of being a better teacher for the equipping of God's people. It *is* worth it.

The good news is that you have an opportunity now — while you're a student — to ensure that Greek is a tool you will be able to use for the rest of your life. If you can develop it now so that it is pretty strong when you go into ministry, it will take a lot less time to keep it ticking along. Reading Greek won't be a laborious struggle because you will know enough to read competently. You won't need to look up every second word or struggle to recognize verbal forms. Reading Greek will be enjoyable and relatively pain-free. And it won't take too much of your time — just a little bit each day. If you can get yourself to that place, you will find it easy to keep your Greek. And that means that you'll have years ahead of you to read the New Testament in Greek, study it in detail, and teach it with depth and understanding.

Summary: It's not rocket science. Get your Greek strong now; keep your Greek strong in the future.

Blog Responses

Michael Kellahan Con, why does all this wise advice sound like my dentist telling me how important daily flossing is?

Mark Stevens Con, my original degree didn't require Greek (something they have since remedied) and so I took a course once I entered ministry. That was a very tough and tiring ride but I made it. How can I get it strong if it has started to slip? Books? Ideas?

Con Campbell Mark, that sounds tough-going. Glad you made it, however.

Michael, I suspect it's because, like the dentist, you know I'm right!

Jason Chamberlain I can say that I really wish that I had done a better job of learning Greek at first. The best thing about the way I handled Greek was that it better prepared me for learning Hebrew. Obviously the languages are very different, but I felt like the mistakes showed me what I needed to do differently when I learned Hebrew. I became much more diligent with vocabulary and I also worked harder to retain the grammar I learned.

Doing it right the first time just makes it much easier.

Con Campbell Thanks for your candour, Jason.

Henry Kirsch I echo Jason's comments; I too regret not learning Greek well the first time. Now as a pastor I'm not sure when I'll get a chance to "do Greek" again. I suppose the unfamiliarity of language acquisition is the greatest hurdle at first. It wasn't until I was out of seminary that I purchased and read *How Biblical Languages Work*. It certainly didn't answer every question, but it's a good place to start to understand the basic concepts of ancient languages.

Next is the hurdle of making language study a discipline. To adequately grasp Greek one needs to turn its study into a habit. Unlike physical exercise, it's a habit of the mind, and if the student can enlist the help of other Greek students for accountability, there is a greater chance for long-term success.

Jason Chamberlain I have had several people make the comment that they wanted to learn Koine Greek. I told them that all they needed was a copy of Mounce, the workbook, and a way to do flashcards and I would be more than happy to help. However, I also give them the same warning that Yoda gave Luke. It's not something that one can do casually.

The funny thing is that Mounce makes an admonition like this at the beginning of BBG, but I didn't really believe it. Looking back, I wish I had taken him more seriously.

Resources

There are plenty of
helpful tools out there.

This resource section provides a sample of the great tools out there — mostly on the Internet — that can help you to keep your Greek. This is not a list of everything available, nor do I claim that these are necessarily the best tools out there. But they certainly are useful, and I recommend them.

General Websites
These websites each contain several useful tools that can be accessed freely.

Institute of Biblical Greek
www.biblicalgreek.org
   This website offers an excellent collection of links to the quality Greek resources around the Internet as well as printed materials. These links include free and commercial software resources, NT and extra-NT texts, and various other learning aids.

Teknia Software
www.learnbiblicalgreek.com/bbg_resources

Bill Mounce has a range of free and commercial resources available on his website. These include a vocabulary drilling program, some songs in Greek, and even Greek bingo!

Resources for Biblical Studies
www.deinde.org/greek.php

Danny Zacharias offers a set of quality resources, including multimedia vocabulary flash cards, more than seventeen songs for the retention of Greek grammar, and some helpful animations to help with morphology.

Forget the Channel
www.lionelwindsor.net/language-tools/greek/

Lionel Windsor has compiled some helpful tools, including a principal parts tester, Greek flash cards in Excel format, and a game similar to *Scrabble* but using Greek vocabulary.

Resources for Reading Greek

A New Reader's Lexicon of the Greek New Testament

This volume by Burer & Miller improves on earlier works and, in canonical order, lists all words occurring fewer than fifty times. In addition to providing the word's definition, this tool includes the number of times a word occurs in a particular author's writings alongside the number of times a word is used in a given book of the New Testament. Not only can this book be used to aid the reading of the Greek New Testament, but it can provide a handy way to learn the rare vocabulary of particular books.

A Reader's Greek New Testament

This Greek New Testament contains footnoted definitions of all Greek words occurring thirty times or less. By knowing the words that occur more than thirty times (and these are listed in a mini-lexicon at the back of the book), the reader can use this Greek New Testament without the need of additional vocabulary aids.

Baylor Handbook on the Greek New Testament
This series of handbooks on the Greek text is in its infancy, but is set to expand rapidly over the next few years. Each handbook provides a convenient reference tool that explains the syntax of the biblical text, offers guidance for deciding between competing semantic analyses, and addresses questions relating to the Greek text that are frequently overlooked or ignored by standard commentaries.

Vocabulary Training Software

ProVoc
www.arizona-software.ch/provoc/
This is a sophisticated software tool for Mac with a rich variety of features. It employs a range of training methods and can be used to learn the vocabulary of many different languages, since it works with user-developed databases. Sam Freney has provided a grammatically tagged database that includes all NT Greek vocabulary grouped according to frequency.

FlashWorks
This is Bill Mounce's vocabulary drilling program, freely available for Mac and PC from the Teknia website (see above).

iVocabulary
http://iphone.chbeer.de/en/iVocabulary/
iVocabulary is a great app for iPhone, which can use the 2500+ databases from *ProVoc*. For example, Sam Freney's *ProVoc* database puts the entire NT vocabulary on your iPhone.

Parsing Software

Paradigmatic

http://paradigmatic.freney.org/

Sam Freney has freely provided a useful Mac application that trains Greek and Hebrew paradigms.

Reading beyond the New Testament

It's a good idea to read Greek outside the New Testament if you can. It will widen your exposure to ancient Greek and will increase your overall reading ability.

Koine Greek Reader

Prepared by Greek scholar Rodney Decker, this book provides graded readings in Koine Greek from the New Testament, Septuagint, Apostolic Fathers, and early creeds. It integrates vocabulary lists, translation helps, basic grammar and syntax, and an introduction to *BDAG*.

Perseus Digital Library

www.perseus.tufts.edu/hopper/

This site has a huge collection of ancient Greek texts that are searchable, with each word linked to an online lexicon (based on LSJ). There is no better site on the Internet for introducing you to reading Greek outside the New Testament.

Basics of Verbal Aspect in Biblical Greek

Constantine R. Campbell

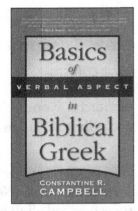

Verbal aspect in the Greek language has been a topic of significant debate in recent scholarship. The majority of scholars now believe that an understanding of verbal aspect is even more important than verb tense (past, present, etc.). Until now, however, there have been no accessible textbooks, both in terms of level and price (most titles on the topic retail for more than $100).

In this book, Constantine Campbell investigates the function of verbal aspect within New Testament Greek narrative. He simplifies the concept without getting caught up in linguistics terms that no one except those schooled in that field can understand. The book includes exercises, an answer key, glossary of key concepts, an appendix probing the issue of space and time, and a subject index and Scripture index.

Professors and students, at both the undergraduate and graduate levels, will use this is as a supplemental text in both beginning and advanced Greek courses. Pastors who study the Greek text will also appreciate this resource as a supplement to their preaching and teaching.

Available in stores and online!

A Reader's Greek New Testament

2nd Edition

Richard J. Goodrich
and Albert L. Lukaszewski

Ideal for Greek students and pastors,
A Reader's Greek New Testament
saves time and effort in studying the Greek New Testament.
By eliminating the need to look up definitions, the footnotes
allow the user to read the Greek text more quickly, focusing
on parsing and grammatical issues. This revised edition offers
the following features:

- New Greek font—easier to read
- Footnoted definitions of all Greek words occurring 30
  times or less
- Mini-lexicon of all words occurring more than 30 times
- Greek text underlying Today's New International
  Version
- Footnotes offering comparisons with UBS4
- 4 pages of full-color maps

Featuring a handsome Italian Duo-Tone™ binding, *A
Reader's Greek New Testament*, 2nd Edition, is a practical,
attractive, and surprisingly affordable resource.

Available in stores and online!

ZONDERVAN®
.com

A Summer Greek Reader

A Workbook for Maintaining Your Biblical Greek

Richard Goodrich
and David Diewert

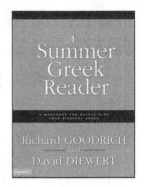

A Summer Greek Reader is the first practical text specifically designed to help students of introductory Greek strengthen their grasp of the essentials over the summer. By spending just twenty minutes a day, students not only maintain what they've learned in their first-year class, but will also build their working vocabulary and gain practice with extended Greek New Testament passages.

This volume is perfect for students who want to begin reading complete passages of the Greek New Testament while avoiding the complexities encountered in intermediate and advanced studies. *A Summer Greek Reader* encourages readers to memorize new words while applying the essentials of Greek to translating larger blocks of the New Testament text.

- Passages are selected for their straightforward syntax.
- Unfamiliar words are cross-referenced or defined in footnotes, eliminating the need for lexical work.
- English translations are provided in the back so students can check their work.

Self-contained and easy to use, *A Summer Greek Reader* is a rewarding means of strengthening the knowledge first-year Greek students have worked so hard to acquire. By eliminating the need to rebuild old foundations and by minimizing the mad dash for a bigger vocabulary during the first weeks of second-year Greek, this book will quickly prove its worth to students and educators alike.

The Basics of New Testament Syntax

An Intermediate
Greek Grammar

Daniel B. Wallace

The Basics of New Testament Syntax provides concise, up-to-date guidance for intermediate Greek students to do accurate exegesis of biblical texts. Abridged from *Greek Grammar beyond the Basics: An Exegetical Syntax of the New Testament*, the popular exegetical Greek grammar for studies in Greek by Daniel B. Wallace, *The Basics of New Testament Syntax* offers a practical grammar for second-year students.

The strengths of this abridgment will become quickly apparent to the user:

- It shows the relevance of syntax for exegesis and is thoroughly cross-referenced to the larger Exegetical Syntax.
- It includes an exceptional number of categories useful for intermediate Greek studies.
- It is easy to use. Each semantic category is discussed, and a definition and key to identification are provided.
- Scores of charts and tables enable the intermediate student to grasp the material quickly.

Available in stores and online!

New International Dictionary of New Testament Theology

Abridged Edition

Verlyn D. Verbrugge

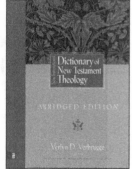

This abridgment of Colin Brown's original four-volume work is arranged with its entries in Greek alphabetical order, which makes it easy to find the discussion of a particular word. All Greek words are transliterated into English and linked with their Goodrick/Kohlenberger numbers. This handy one-volume theological dictionary summarizes the heart of larger work and is perfect for word studies and theological reflection.